The Wisdom of No Escape

and the Path of Loving-Kindness

PEMA CHÖDRÖN

SHAMBHALA
Boston & London
2010

Frontispiece: Photo by Nancy Jo Johnson

Shambhala Publications, Inc.
Horticultural Hall
300 Massachusetts Avenue
Boston, Massachusetts 02115
www.shambhala.com

The author's proceeds from this book will be donated to Gampo
Abbey, Pleasant Bay, Nova Scotia.

9 8 7 6 5 4 3 2

PRINTED IN CHINA

⊗This edition is printed on acid-free paper that meets the
American National Standards Institute z39.48 Standard.
♻Shambhala Publications makes every effort to print on recycled paper.
For more information please visit www.shambhala.com.
Distributed in the United States by Random House, Inc.,
and in Canada by Random House of Canada Ltd

*The Library of Congress catalogues the original edition
of this book as follows:*

Chödron, Pema.
The wisdom of no escape: and the path of loving-kindness/
Pema Chödrön.
p. cm.
ISBN 978-0-87773-632-5 (pbk.: alk. paper)
ISBN 978-1-57062-872-6 (pbk.)
ISBN 978-1-59030-793-9 (Shambhala Library)
1. Meditation—Buddhism. I. Title.
BQ5625.C48 1991
294.3´443—dc20 90-53585 CIP

To my teacher,
Vidyadhara the Venerable
Chogyam Trungpa, Rinpoche,
and to my children, Arlyn and Edward

CONTENTS

PREFACE

THE TALKS in this book were given during a one-month practice period *(dathun)* in the spring of 1989. During that month the participants, both lay and monastic, used the meditation technique presented by Chögyam Trungpa that is described in this book. The formal sitting meditation was balanced by walking meditation and eating meditation *(oryoki)* and by maintaining the environment of the monastery and helping to prepare the meals.

Early each morning these talks were presented. They were intended to inspire and encourage the participants to remain wholeheartedly awake to everything that occurred and to use the abundant material of daily life as their primary teacher and guide.

The natural beauty of Gampo Abbey, a Buddhist monastery for Western men and women founded in 1983 by Chögyam Trungpa, was an important element in the talks. The abbey is located on Cape Breton Island, Nova Scotia, at the end of a long dirt road, on cliffs high above the Gulf of Saint Lawrence, where the wildness and playfulness of the weather, the animals, and the landscape permeate the atmosphere. As one sits in the meditation hall, the vastness of the sky and water permeates the mind and heart. The silence of the place, intensified by the sounds of sea and wind, birds and animals, permeates the senses.

During the dathun (as always at the abbey), the participants kept the five monastic vows: not to lie, not to steal, not to engage in sexual activity, not to take life, and not to use alcohol or drugs.

The resulting collaboration of nature, solitude, meditation, and vows made an alternatingly painful and delightful "no exit" situation. With nowhere to hide, one could more easily hear the teachings given in these simple talks in a wholehearted, open-minded way.

The message for the dathun as well as for the reader is to be with oneself without embarrassment or harshness. This is instruction on how to love oneself and one's world. It is therefore simple, accessible instruction on how to alleviate human misery at a personal and global level.

I wish to thank Ane Trime Lhamo; Jonathan Green of Shambhala Publications, who encouraged me to publish a book; Migme Chödrön of Gampo Abbey, who transcribed and edited the talks; and Emily Hilburn Sell of Shambhala Publications, who shaped them into their present form. Whatever is said here is but my very limited understanding, thus far, of what my teacher, Chögyam Trungpa, Rinpoche, compassionately and with great patience showed to me.

May it be of benefit.

The Wisdom of No Escape

I

Loving-Kindness

THERE'S A COMMON misunderstanding among all the human beings who have ever been born on the earth that the best way to live is to try to avoid pain and just try to get comfortable. You can see this even in insects and animals and birds. All of us are the same.

A much more interesting, kind, adventurous, and joyful approach to life is to begin to develop our curiosity, not caring whether the object of our inquisitiveness is bitter or sweet. To lead a life that goes beyond pettiness and prejudice and always wanting to make sure that everything turns out on our own terms, to lead a more passionate, full, and delightful life than that, we must realize that we can endure a lot of pain and pleasure for the sake of finding out who we are and what this world is, how we tick and how our world ticks, how the whole thing just *is*. If we're committed to comfort at any cost, as soon as we come up against the least edge of pain, we're going to run; we'll never know what's beyond that particular barrier or wall or fearful thing.

When people start to meditate or to work with any kind of spiritual discipline, they often think that somehow they're going to improve, which is a sort of subtle aggression against who they really are. It's a bit like saying, "If I jog, I'll be a much better person." "If I could only get a nicer house, I'd be a better person." "If I could meditate and calm down, I'd be a better person." Or the scenario may be that they find fault with others; they might say, "If it weren't for my husband, I'd have a perfect marriage." "If it weren't for the fact that my boss and I can't get on, my job would be just great." And "If it weren't for my mind, my meditation would be excellent."

But loving-kindness—*maitri*—toward ourselves doesn't mean getting rid of anything. Maitri means that we can still be crazy after all these years. We can still be angry after all these years. We can still be timid or jealous or full of feelings of unworthiness. The point is not to try to change ourselves. Meditation practice isn't about trying to throw ourselves away and become something better. It's about befriending who we are already. The ground of practice is you or me or whoever we are right now, just as we are. That's the ground, that's what we study, that's what we come to know with tremendous curiosity and interest.

Sometimes among Buddhists the word *ego* is used in a derogatory sense, with a different connotation than the Freudian term. As Buddhists, we might say, "My ego causes me so many problems." Then we might think, "Well, then, we're supposed to get rid of it, right? Then there'd be no problem." On the contrary, the idea isn't to get rid of ego but actually to begin to take an interest in ourselves, to investigate and be inquisitive about ourselves.

The path of meditation and the path of our lives altogether has to do with curiosity, inquisitiveness. The ground is ourselves; we're here to study ourselves and to get to know ourselves now, not later. People often say to me, "I wanted to come and have an interview with you, I wanted to write you a letter, I wanted to call you on the phone, but I wanted to wait until I was more together." And I think, "Well, if you're anything like me, you could wait forever!" So come as you are. The magic is being willing to open to that, being willing to be fully awake to that. One of the main discoveries of meditation is seeing how we continually run away from the present moment, how we avoid being here just as we are. That's not considered to be a problem; the point is to see it.

Inquisitiveness or curiosity involves being gentle, precise, and open—actually being able to let go and open. Gentleness is a sense of goodheartedness toward ourselves. Precision is being able to see very clearly, not being afraid to see what's really there, just as a scientist is not afraid to look into the microscope. Openness is being able to let go and to open.

The effect of this month of meditation that we are beginning will be as if, at the end of each day, someone were to play a video of you back to yourself and you could see it all. You would wince quite often and say "Ugh!" You probably would see that you do all those things for which you criticize all those people you don't like in your life, all those people that you judge. Basically, making friends with yourself is making friends with all those people too, because when you come to have this kind of honesty, gentleness, and goodheartedness, combined with clarity about yourself, there's no obstacle to feeling loving-kindness for others as well.

So the ground of maitri is ourselves. We're here to get to know and study ourselves. The path, the way to do that, our main vehicle, is going to be meditation, and some sense of general wakefulness. Our inquisitiveness will not be limited just to sitting here; as we walk through the halls, use the lavatories, walk outdoors, prepare food in the kitchen, or talk to our friends—whatever we do—we will try to maintain that sense of aliveness, openness, and curiosity about what's happening. Perhaps we will experience what is traditionally described as the fruition of maitri— playfulness.

So hopefully we'll have a good month here, getting to know ourselves and becoming more playful, rather than more grim.

2

Satisfaction

I T'S VERY HELPFUL to realize that being here, sitting in meditation, doing simple everyday things like working, walking outside, talking with people, bathing, using the toilet, and eating, is actually all that we need to be fully awake, fully alive, fully human. It's also helpful to realize that this body that we have, this very body that's sitting here right now on this shrine room floor, this very body that perhaps aches because it's only day two of the dathun, and this mind that we have at this very moment, are exactly what we need to be fully human, fully awake, and fully alive. Furthermore, the emotions that we have right now, the negativity and the positivity, are what we actually need. It is just as if we had looked around to find out what would be the greatest wealth that we could possibly possess in order to lead a decent, good, completely fulfilling, energetic, inspired life, and found it all right here.

Being satisfied with what we already have is a magical golden key to being alive in a full, unrestricted, and inspired way. One of the major obstacles to what is traditionally called enlightenment is resentment, feeling cheated, holding a grudge about who you are, where you are, what you are. This is why we talk so much about making friends with ourselves, because, for some reason or other, we don't feel that kind of satisfaction in a full and complete way. Meditation is a process of lightening up, of trusting the basic goodness of what we have and who we are, and of realizing that any wisdom that exists, exists in what we already have. Our wisdom is all mixed up with what we call our neurosis. Our brilliance, our juiciness, our spiciness, is all mixed up with our craziness and our confusion, and therefore it doesn't do any good to try to get rid of our so-called negative aspects, because in that process we also get rid of our basic wonderfulness. We can lead our life so as to become more awake to who we are and what we're doing rather than trying to improve or change or get rid of who we are or what we're doing. The key is to wake up, to become more alert, more inquisitive and curious about ourselves.

While we are sitting in meditation, we are simply exploring humanity and all of creation in the form of ourselves. We can become the world's greatest experts on anger, jealousy, and self-deprecation, as well as on joyfulness, clarity, and insight. Everything that human beings feel, we feel. We can become extremely wise and sensitive to all of humanity and the whole universe simply by knowing ourselves, just as we are.

We're talking about loving-kindness again, in a slightly different way. The ground of loving-kindess is this sense of satisfaction with who we are and what we have. The path is a sense of wonder, becoming a two- or three-year-old child again, wanting to know all the unknowable things, beginning to question everything. We know we're never really going to find the answers, because these kinds of questions come from having a hunger and a passion for life—they have nothing to do with resolving anything or tying it all up into a neat little package. This kind of questioning is the journey itself. The fruition lies in beginning to realize our kinship with all humanity. We realize that we have a share in whatever everyone else has and is. Our journey of making friends with ourselves is not a selfish thing. We're not trying to get all the goodies for ourselves. It's a process of developing loving-kindness and a true understanding for other people as well.

3
Finding Our Own True Nature

IN ONE OF the Buddha's discourses, he talks about the four kinds of horses: the excellent horse, the good horse, the poor horse, and the really bad horse. The excellent horse, according to the sutra,* moves before the whip even touches its back; just the shadow of the whip or the slightest sound from the driver is enough to make the horse move. The good horse runs at the lightest touch of the whip on its back. The poor horse doesn't go until it feels pain, and the very bad horse doesn't budge until the pain penetrates to the marrow of its bones.

When Shunryu Suzuki tells the story in his book *Zen Mind, Beginner's Mind,* he says that when people hear this sutra, they always want to be the best horse, but actually, when we sit, it doesn't matter whether we're the best horse or the worst horse. He goes on to say that in fact, the really terrible horse is the best practitioner.

What I have realized through practicing is that

---

*A discourse or teaching by the Buddha.

practice isn't about being the best horse or the good horse or the poor horse or the worst horse. It's about finding our own true nature and speaking from that, acting from that. Whatever our quality is, that's our wealth and our beauty; that's what other people respond to.

Once I had an opportunity to talk with Chögyam Trungpa, Rinpoche, about the fact that I was not able to do my practice properly. I had just started the vajrayana* practices and I was supposed to be visualizing. I couldn't visualize anything. I tried and tried but there was just nothing at all; I felt like a fraud doing the practice because it didn't feel natural to me. I was quite miserable because everybody else seemed to be having all kinds of visualizations and doing very well. He said, "I'm always suspicious of the ones who say everything's going well. If you think that things are going well, then it's usually some kind of arrogance. If it's too easy for you, you just relax. You don't make a real effort, and therefore you never find out what it is to be fully human." So he encouraged me by saying that as long as you have these kinds of doubts, your practice will be good. When you begin to think that everything is just perfect and feel complacent and superior to the others, watch out!

Dainin Katagiri Roshi once told a story about his own experience of being the worst horse. When he

---

*The "diamond vehicle." The practice of taking the result as the path.

first came to the United States from Japan, he was a young monk in his late twenties. He had been a monk in Japan—where everything was so precise, so clean, and so neat—for a long time. In the U.S., his students were hippies with long, unwashed hair and ragged clothes and no shoes. He didn't like them. He couldn't help it—he just couldn't stand those hippies. Their style offended everything in him. He said, "So all day I would give talks about compassion, and at night I would go home and weep and cry because I realized I had no compassion at all. Because I didn't like my students, therefore I had to work much harder to develop my heart." As Suzuki Roshi says in his talk, that's exactly the point: because we find ourselves to be the worst horse, we are inspired to try harder.

At Gampo Abbey we had a Tibetan monk, Lama Sherap Tendar, teaching us to play the Tibetan musical instruments. We had forty-nine days in which to learn the music; we were also going to learn many other things, we thought, during that time. But as it turned out, for forty-nine days, twice a day, all we did was learn to play the cymbals and the drum and how they are played together. Every day we would practice and practice. We would practice on our own, and then we would play for Lama Sherap, who would sit there with this pained little look on his face. Then he would take our hands and show us how to play. Then we would do it by ourselves, and he would sigh. This went on for forty-nine days. He never said that we were doing well, but he was very sweet and very gentle. Finally, when it was all over and we had had our last performance, we were making toasts and remarks and Lama Sherap said, "Actually you were very good. You were very good right from the beginning, but I knew if I told you that you were good, you would stop trying." He was right. He had such a gentle way of encouraging us that it didn't make us angry with him and it didn't make us lose heart. It just made us feel that he knew the proper way to play the cymbals; he'd been playing these cymbals since he was a little boy, and we just had to keep trying. So for forty-nine days we really worked hard.

We can work with ourselves in the same way. We don't have to be harsh with ourselves when we think, sitting here, that our medittion or our oryoki or the way we are. in the world is in the category of worst horse. We could be very sympathetic with that and use it as a motivation to keep trying to develop ourselves, to find our own true nature. Not only will we find our own true nature, but we'll learn about other people, because in our heart of hearts almost all of us feel that we are the worst horse. You might consider that you yourself are an arrogant person or you might consider that someone else is an arrogant person, but everybody who has ever felt even a moment of arrogance knows that arrogance is just a cover-up for really feeling that you're the worst horse, and always trying to prove otherwise.

In his talk, Suzuki Roshi says that meditation and the whole process of finding your own true nature is one continuous mistake, and that rather than that being a reason for depression or discouragement, it's actually the motivation. When you find yourself slumping, that's the motivation to sit up, not out of self-denigration but actually out of pride in everything that occurs to you, pride in who you are just as you are, pride in the goodness or the fairness or the worstness of yourself—however you find yourself—some sort of sense of taking pride and using it to spur you on.

The Karma Kagyü lineage of Tibetan Buddhism, in which the students of Chögyam Trungpa are trained, is sometimes called the "mishap lineage," because of the ways in which the wise and venerated teachers of this lineage "blew it" time after time. First there was Tilopa, who was a madman, completely wild. His main student was Naropa. Naropa was so conceptual and intellectual that it took him twelve years of being run over by a truck, of being put through all sorts of trials by his teacher, for him to begin to wake up. He was so conceptual that if somebody would tell him something, he would say, "Oh yes, but surely by *that* you must mean *this*." He had that kind of mind. His main student was Marpa, who was famous for his intensely bad temper. He used to fly into rages, beat people, and yell at them. He was also a drunk. He was notorious for being incredibly stubborn. His student was Milarepa. Milarepa was a murderer! Rinpoche used to say that Marpa became a student of the dharma because he thought he could make a lot of money by bringing texts back from India and translating them into Tibetan. His student Milarepa became a student because he was afraid he was going to go to hell for having murdered people— that scared him.

Milarepa's student· was Gampopa (after whom Gampo Abbey is named). Because everything was easy for him, Gampopa was arrogant. For instance, the night before he met Gampopa for the first time, Milarepa said to some of his disciples, "Oh, someone who is destined to be my main student is going to come tomorrow. Whoever brings him to me will be greatly benefited." So when Gampopa arrived in the town, an old lady who saw him ran out and said, "Oh, Milarepa told us you were coming and that you were destined to be one of his main students, and I want my daughter to bring you to see him." So Gampopa, thinking, "I must be really hot stuff," went very proudly to meet Milarepa, sure that he would be greeted with great honor. However, Milarepa had had someone put him in a cave and wouldn't see Gampopa for three weeks.

As for Gampopa's main student, the first Karmapa, the only thing we know aout him is that he was extremely ugly. He was said to look like a monkey. Also, there's one story about him and three other main disciples of Gampopa who were thrown out of the monastery for getting drunk and singing and dancing and breaking the monastic rules.

We could all take heart. These are the wise ones who sit in front of us, to whom we prostrate when we do prostrations. We can prostrate to them as an example of our own wisdom mind of enlightened beings, but perhaps it's also good to prostrate to them as confused, mixed-up people with a lot of neurosis, just like ourselves. They are good examples of people who never gave up on themselves and were not afraid to be themselves, who therefore found their own genuine quality and their own true nature.

The point is that our true nature is not some ideal that we have to live up to. It's who we are right now, and that's what we can make friends with and celebrate.

4

Precision, Gentleness, and Letting Go

IN MEDITATION and in our daily lives there are three qualities that we can nurture, cultivate, and bring out. We already possess these, but they can be ripened: precision, gentleness, and the ability to let go.

When the Buddha taught, he didn't say that we were bad people or that there was some sin that we had committed—original or otherwise—that made us more ignorant than clear, more harsh than gentle, more closed than open. He taught that there is a kind of innocent misunderstanding that we all share, something that can be turned around, corrected, and seen through, as if we were in a dark room and someone showed us where the light switch was. It isn't a sin that we are in the dark room. It's just an innocent situation, but how fortunate that someone shows us where the light switch is. It brightens up our life considerably. We can start to read books, to see one another's faces, to discover the colors of the walls, to enjoy the little animals that creep in and out of the room.

In the same way, if we see our so-called limitations

with clarity, precision, gentleness, goodheartedness, and kindness and, having seen them fully, then let go, open further, we begin to find that our world is more vast and more refreshing and fascinating than we had realized before. In other words, the key to feeling more whole and less shut off and shut down is to be able to see clearly who we are and what we're doing.

The innocent mistake that keeps us caught in our own particular style of ignorance, unkindness, and shut-downness is that we are never encouraged to see clearly what is, with gentleness. Instead, there's a kind of basic misunderstanding that we should try to be better than we already are, that we should try to improve ourselves, that we should try to get away from painful things, and that if we could just learn how to get away from the painful things, then we would be happy. That is the innocent, naive misunderstanding that we all share, which keeps us unhappy.

Meditation is about seeing clearly the body that we have, the mind that we have, the domestic situation that we have, the job that we have, and the people who are in our lives. It's about seeing how we react to all these things. It's seeing our emotions and thoughts just as they are right now, in this very moment, in this very room, on this very seat. It's about not trying to make them go away, not trying to become better than we are, but just seeing clearly with precision and gentleness. Throughtout this month of meditation practice, we will work with cultivating gentleness, innate precision, and the ability to let go of small-mindedness, learning how to open to our thoughts and emotions, to all the people we meet in our world, how to open our minds and hearts.

This is not an improvement plan; it is not a situation in which you try to be better than you are now. If you have a bad temper and you feel that you harm yourself and others, you might think that sitting for a week or a month will make your bad temper go away—you will be that sweet person that you always wanted to be. Never again will a harsh word leave your lily-white lips. The problem is that the desire to change is fundamentally a form of aggression toward yourself. The other problem is that our hangups, unfortunately or fortunately, contain our wealth. Our neurosis and our wisdom are made out of the same material. If you throw out your neurosis, you also throw out your wisdom. Someone who is very angry also has a lot of energy; that energy is what's so juicy about him or her. That's the reason people love that person. The idea isn't to try to get rid of your anger, but to make friends with it, to see it clearly with precision and honesty, and also to see it with gentleness. That means not judging yourself as a bad person, but also not bolstering yourself up by saying, "It's good that I'm this way, it's right that I'm this way. Other people are terrible, and I'm right to be so angry at them all the time." The gentleness involves not repressing the anger but also not acting it out. It is something much softer and more openhearted than any of that. It involves learning how, once you have fully acknowledged the feeling of anger and the knowledge of who you are and what you do, to let it go. You can let go of the usual pitiful little story line that accompanies anger and begin to see clearly how you keep the whole thing going. So whether it's anger or craving or jealousy or fear or depression—whatever it might be—the notion is not to try to get rid of it, but to make friends with it. That means getting to know it completely, with some kind of softness, and learning how, once you've experienced it fully, to let go.

The meditation technique itself cultivates precision, gentleness, and the ability to let go—qualities that are innate within us. They are not something that we have to gain, but something that we could bring out, cultivate, rediscover in ourselves. Now I'd like to discuss the meditation technique and point out how it helps bring out these qualities.

Precision

The technique is, first, to take good posture and, second, to become mindful of your out-breath. This is just your ordinary out-breath, not manipulated or controlled in any way. Be with the breath as it goes out, feel the breath go out, touch the breath as it goes out. Now, this seems simple, but to actually be with that breath and to be there for every breath requires a lot of precision. When you sit down and begin to meditate, the fact that you always come back to that breath brings out the precision, the clarity, and the accuracy of your mind. Just the fact that you always come back to this breath and that you try, in a gentle way, to be as fully with the breath as you can sharpens your mind.

The third part of the technique is that, when you realize that you've been thinking, you say to yourself, "Thinking." Now, that also requires a lot of precision. Even if you wake up as if from a dream and realize that you've been thinking, and you immediately go back to the breath and accidentally forget about the labeling, even then you should just pause a little bit and say to yourself, "Thinking." Use the label, because the label is so precise. Just acknowledge that you've been thinking, just that, no more, no less, just "thinking." Being with the out-breath cultivates the precision of your mind, and when you label, that too brings out the precision of your mind. Your mind becomes more clear and stabilized. As you sit, you might want to be aware of this.

Gentleness

If we emphasized only precision, our meditation might become quite harsh and militant. It might get too goal-oriented. So we also emphasize gentleness.

One thing that is very helpful is to cultivate an over-all sense of relaxation while you are doing the meditation. I think you'll notice that as you become more mindful and more aware and awake, you begin to notice that your stomach tends to get very tense and your shoulders tend to get very tight. It helps a lot if you notice this and then purposely relax your stomach, relax your shoulders and your neck. If you find it difficult to relax, just gradually, patiently, gently work with it.

When the breath goes out, not only does it ripen the precision of our minds, but it also brings out this inherent gentle quality, this quality of heart or warmth, of kindness, because the attention to the breath is very soft. If you were doing a technique that said, "Concentrate on the out-breath, have one hundred percent attention on the out-breath" (and there are techniques like that which are very beneficial), that would be cultivating precision, but not gentleness. But since this technique is ripening not only precision, but also gentleness, the instruction is that there is only twenty-five percent awareness on the out-breath, which is really very little. The truth of the matter is that if you are concentrating on the out-breath and *only* on the out-breath, you're not being aware of the person next to you, of the lights going on and off, of the sound of the ocean. However, in this technique, because your eyes are open and because the gaze is not a tight gaze and because the whole emphasis of the practice is one of openness, even though you're mindful of the out-breath, you're not shutting out all the other things that are going on. So it's only twenty-five percent awareness on the out-breath. The other awareness is less specific; it's simply that you are alive in this room with all the different things that are occurring here. So we give the instruction, "Be mindful of your out-breath, be with your out-breath," and that's what you do. But the instruction that the awareness is only twenty-five percent really brings home the idea that it's not a concentration practice—there's a very light touch on the breath as it goes out. Touch the breath and let it go. The touch is the precision part and also the softness part. Touch it very softly and let it go.

If the object of meditation were something concrete, something solid and graspable—an image or a statue or a dot on the floor or a candle—it would be much more of a concentration exercise. But the breath is very elusive; even if you wanted to give it one hundred percent attention, it would be difficult because it is so ephemeral, so light, so airy and spacious. As the object of meditation, it brings a sense of softness and gentleness. It's like being mindful of a gentle breeze, but in this case it's our ordinary, uncontrived out-breath. This technique with the breath is said to be without a goal. You are not doing it to achieve anything except to be fully present. Being fully present isn't something that happens once and then you have achieved it; it's being awake to the ebb and flow and movement and creation of life, being alive to the process of life itself. That also has its softness. If there were a goal that you were supposed to achieve, such as "no thoughts," that wouldn't be very soft. You'd have to struggle a lot to get rid of all those thoughts, and you probably couldn't do it anyway. The fact that there is no goal also adds to the softness.

The moment when you label your thoughts "thinking" is probably the key place in the technique where you cultivate gentleness, sympathy, and loving-kindness. Rinpoche used to say, "Notice your tone of voice when you say 'thinking.'" It might be really harsh, but actually it's just a euphemism for "Drat! You were thinking again, gosh darn it, you dummy." You might really be saying, "You fool, you absolutely miserable meditator, you're hopeless." But it's not that at all. All that's happened is that you've noticed. Good for you, you actually noticed! You've noticed that mind thinks continuously, and it's wonderful that you've seen that. Having seen it, let the thoughts go. Say, "Thinking." If you notice that you're being harsh, say it a second time just to cultivate the feeling that you could say it to yourself with gentleness and kindness, in other words, that you are cultivating a nonjudgmental attitude. You are not criticizing yourself, you are just seeing what *is* with precision and gentleness, seeing thinking as thinking. That is how this technique cultivates not only precision but also softness, gentleness, a sense of warmth toward oneself. The honesty of precision and the goodheartedness of gentleness are qualities of making friends with yourself. So during this period, along with being as precise as you can, really emphasize the softness. If you find your body tensing, relax it. If you find your mind tensing, relax it. Feel the expansiveness of the breath going out into the space. When thoughts come up, touch them very lightly, like a feather touching a bubble. Let the whole thing be soft and gentle, but at the same time precise.

Letting Go

The third aspect of the technique is the quality of opening or letting go. This seemingly simple technique helps us rediscover this ability that we already have to open beyond small-mindedness and to let go of any kind of fixation or limited view. Precision and gentleness are somewhat tangible. You can work on being more accurate with the out-breath, more accurate with the label. You can relax your stomach and your shoulders and your body, and you can be softer with the out-breath and more sympathetic with the labeling. But letting go is not so easy. Rather, it's something that happens as a result of working with precision and gentleness. In other words, as you work with being really faithful to the technique and being as precise as you can and simultaneously as kind as you can, the ability to let go seems to happen to you. The discovery of your ability to let go spontaneously arises; you don't force it. You shouldn't be forcing accuracy or gentleness either, but while you *could* make a project out of accuracy, you *could* make a project out of gentleness, it's hard to make a project out of letting go. Nevertheless, I'll describe how the technique leads you toward this rediscovery of your ability to let go and to open.

You may have wondered why we are mindful of our out-breath and only our out-breath. Why don't we pay attention to the out-breath *and* the in-breath? There are other excellent techniques that instruct the meditator to be mindful of the breath going out and mindful of the breath coming in. That definitely sharpens the mind and brings a sense of one-pointed, continuous mindfulness, with no break in it. But in this meditation technique, we are with the out-breath; there's no particular instruction about what to do until the next out-breath. Inherent in this technique is the ability to let go at the end of the out-breath, to open at the end of the out-breath, because for a moment there's actually no instruction about what to do. There's a possibility of what Rinpoche used to call "gap" at the end of the out-breath: you're mindful of your breath as it goes out, and then there's a pause as the breath comes in. It's as if you . . . pause. It doesn't help at all to say, "Don't be mindful of the in-breath"—that's like saying, "Don't think of a pink elephant." When you're told not to be mindful of something, it becomes an obsession. Nevertheless, the mindfulness is on the out-breath, and there's some sense of just waiting for the next out-breath, a sense of no project. One could just let go at the end of the out-breath. Breath goes out and dissolves, and there could be some sense of letting go completely. Nothing to hold on to until the next out-breath.

Even though it's difficult to do, as you begin to work with mindfulness of the out-breath, then the pause, just waiting, and then mindfulness of the next out-breath, the sense of being able to let go gradually begins to dawn on you. So you don't have any high expectations—just do the technique. As the months and years go by, the way you regard the world will begin to change. You will learn what it is to let go and what it is to open beyond limited beliefs and ideas about things.

The experience of labeling your thoughts "thinking" also, over time, becomes much more vivid. You may be completely caught up in a fantasy, in remembering the past or planning for the future, completely caught up, as if you had gotten on an airplane and flown away someplace. You're elsewhere and you are with other people and you've redecorated a room or you've relived a pleasant or unpleasant experience or you've gotten all caught up in worrying about something that might happen or you're getting a lot of pleasure from thinking about something that may happen, but you're completely involved as if in a dream. Then suddenly you realize, and you just come back. It happens automatically. You say to yourself, "Thinking," and as you're saying that, basically what you are doing is letting go of those thoughts. You don't repress the thoughts. You acknowledge them as "thinking" very clearly and kindly, but then you let them go. Once you begin to get the hang of this, it's incredibly powerful that you could be completely obsessed with hope and fear and all kinds of other thoughts and you could realize what you've been doing—without criticizing it—and you could let it go. This is probably one of the most amazing tools that you could be given, the ability to just let things go, not to be caught in the grip of your own angry thoughts of passionate thoughts or worried thoughts or depressed thoughts.

5
The Wisdom of No Escape

YESTERDAY I talked about cultivating precision, gentleness, and openness, and described how the meditation technique helps us remember the qualities that we already possess. Now, sometimes the teachings emphasize the wisdom, brilliance, or sanity that we possess, and sometimes they emphasize the obstacles, how it is that we feel stuck in a small, dark place. These are actually two sides of one coin: when they are put together, inspiration (or well-being) and burden (or suffering) describe the human condition. That's what we see when we meditate.

We see how beautiful and wonderful and amazing things are, and we see how caught up we are. It isn't that one is the bad part and one is the good part, but that it's a kind of interesting, smelly, rich, fertile mess of stuff. When it's all mixed up together, it's us: humanness. This is what we are here to see for ourselves. Both the brilliance and the suffering are here all the time; they interpenetrate each other. For a fully enlightened being, the difference between what is neurosis and what is wisdom is very hard to perceive, because somehow the energy underlying both of them is the same. The basic creative energy of life—life force—bubbles up and courses through all of existence. It can be experienced as open, free, unburdened, full of possibility, energizing. Or this very same energy can be experienced as petty, narrow, stuck, caught. Even though there are so many teachings, so many meditations, so many instructions, the basic point of it all is just to learn to be extremely honest and also wholehearted about what exists in your mind—thoughts, emotions, bodily sensations, the whole thing that adds up to what we call "me" or "I." Nobody else can really begin to sort out for you what to accept and what to reject in terms of what wakes you up and what makes you fall asleep. No one else can really sort out for you what to accept— what opens up your world—and what to reject— what seems to keep you going round and round in some kind of repetitive misery. This meditation is called nontheistic, which doeesn't have anything to do with believing in God or not believing in God, but means that nobody but yourself can tell you what to accept and what to reject.

The practice of meditation helps us get to know this basic energy really well, with tremendous honesty and warmheartedness, and we begin to figure out for ourselves what is poison and what is medicine, which means something different for each of us. For example, some people can drink a lot of coffee and it really wakes them up and they feel great; others can drink just a thimbleful and become a nervous wreck.

Everything we eat affects each of us differently; so it is with how we relate with our own energies. We are the only ones who know what wakes us up and what puts us to sleep. So we sit here on these red cushions in this brightly lit room with this fancy, colorful shrine and this huge picture of the Karmapa. Outside, the snow is falling and the wind howling. Hour after hour we sit here and just come back to the present moment as much as we can, acknowledge what's going on in our minds, come back to the present moment as much as we can, acknowledge what's going on in our minds, follow the out-breath, label our thoughts "thinking," come back to the present moment, acknowledge what's going on in our minds. The instruction is to be as honest and warmhearted in the process as you can, to learn gradually what it means to let go of holding on and holding back.

The message is that each of us has all that it takes to become fully enlightened. We have basic energy coursing through us. Sometimes it manifests as brilliance and sometimes it manifests as confusion. Because we are decent, basically good people, we ourselves can sort out what to accept and what to reject. We can discern what will make us complete, sane, grown-up people, and what—if we are too involved in it—will keep us children forever. This is the process of making friends with ourselves and with our world. It involves not just the parts we like, but the whole picture, because it all has a lot to teach us.

6
Joy

ALMOST A YEAR AGO, a dear friend of ours, Sister Ayya Khema, a German woman who is a Theravadin nun living in Sri Lanka, came to visit us and to lead a *vipashyana* (insight meditation) retreat. The retreat for me personally was something of a revelation, because she emphasized joy. I hadn't realized how much emphasis I had put on suffering in my own practice. I had focused on coming to terms with the unpleasant, unacceptable, embarrassing, and painful things that I do. In the process, I had very subtly forgotten about joy.

In our seven-day silent retreat, Ayya Khema taught us that each of us has in our heart a joy that's accessible to us; by connecting to it and letting it flower, we allow ourselves to celebrate our practice and our lives. Joy is like a soft spring rain that allows us to lighten up, to enjoy ourselves, and therefore it's a whole new way of looking at suffering.

In a little book called *A Guide to Walking Meditation,* in the chapter "The World Contains All the Wonders of the Pure Land," Thich Nhat Hanh says, "I don't think that all the Buddhas and Bodhisattvas of the three times will criticize me for giving you a little secret, that there is no need to go somewhere else to find the wonders of the Pure Land." That sense of wonder and delight is present in every moment, every breath, every step, every movement of our own ordinary everyday lives, if we can connect with it. The greatest obstacle to connecting with our joy is resentment.

Joy has to do with seeing how big, how completely unobstructed, and how precious things are. Resenting what happens to you and complaining about your life are like refusing to smell the wild roses when you go for a morning walk, or like being so blind that you don't see a huge black raven when it lands in the tree that you're sitting under. We can get so caught up in our own personal pain or worries that we don't notice that the wind has come up or that somebody has put flowers on the diningroom table or that when we walked out in the morning, the flags weren't up, and that when we came back, they were flying. Resentment, bitterness, and holding a grudge prevent us from seeing and hearing and tasting and delighting.

There is a story of a woman running away from tigers. She runs and runs, and the tigers are getting closer and closer. When she comes to the edge of a cliff, she sees some vines there, so she climbs down and holds on to the vines. Looking down, she sees that there are tigers below her as well. She then notices that a mouse is gnawing away at the vine to which she is clinging. She also sees a beautiful little bunch of strawberries close to her, growing out of a clump of grass. She looks up and she looks down. She looks at the mouse. Then she takes a strawberry, puts it in her mouth, and enjoys it thoroughly.

Tigers above, tigers below. This is actually the predicament that we are always in, in terms of our birth and death. Each moment is just what it is. It might be the only moment of our life, it might be the only strawberry we'll ever eat. We could get depressed about it, or we could finally appreciate it and delight in the preciousness of every single moment of our life.

Trungpa Rinpoche always used to say, "You can do it." That was probably one of his main teachings, "You can do it." Thich Nhat Hanh, in his *Guide to Walking Meditation,* begins by talking about how everybody carries around this burden, and if you want to put it off, if you want to lay it down, you *can* do it. You *can* connect with the joy in your heart.

On a day of silence like today, when things are very still, you may find that you are feeling grim and doing everything with a grim expression: grimly opening the door, grimly drinking your tea, concentrating so hard on being quiet and still and moving slowly that you're miserable. On the other hand, you could just relax and realize that, behind all the worry, complaint, and disapproval that goes on in your mind, the sun is always coming up in the morning, moving across the sky, and going down in the evening. The birds are always out there collecting their food and making

their nests and flying across the sky. The grass is always being blown by the wind or standing still. Food
and flowers and trees are growing out of the earth.
There's enormous richness. You could develop your
passion for life and your curiosity and your interest.
You could connect with your joyfulness. You could
start right now.

The Navajo teach their children that every morning when the sun comes up, it's a brand-new sun. It's
born each morning, it lives for the duration of one
day, and in the evening it passes on, never to return
again. As soon as the children are old enough to understand, the adults take them out at dawn and they
say, "The sun has only one day. You must live this day
in a good way, so that the sun won't have wasted precious time." Acknowledging the preciousness of each
day is a good way to live, a good way to reconnect
with our basic joy.

7
Taking a Bigger Perspective

THIS MORNING when I came to meditation I was hungry and tired; I was also happy. When we took the morning walk, I felt even happier, and I realized it had to do with something that happens to us when we practice: we find that we have a bigger perspective on our lives. This feels almost like a blessing or a gift.

In many traditions, including Tibetan Buddhism, the circle is a powerful symbol for the sacredness of all things. Throughout these traditions, there are rituals in which the image of the circle is used like this: by drawing a circle around yourself and standing in the middle of it, you realize that you are always at the center of the universe. The circle that surrounds you shows you that you're always in the sacred space.

In Buddhism we talk about mindfulness and awareness. We're taught mindfulness through oryoki, and through bowing, and through being with the breath, labeling our thoughts "thinking." There's a lot of precision, but also a lot of gentleness. Along with being very precise about our world, there's also always space around us that is called gentleness: we allow ourselves to experience how large and fluid and full of color and energy our world is. This space is our circle.

When we talk about mindfulness and awareness, we're not talking about something stern, a discipline that we impose on ourselves so that we can clean up our act and be better and stand up straighter and smell nicer. It's more that we practice some sense of loving-kindness toward microphones and oryoki bowls and our hands and each other and this room and all the doors we go in and out of. Mindfulness is loving all the details of our lives, and awareness is the natural thing that happens: life begins to open up, and you realize that you're always standing at the center of the world.

Some of you may have read a book called *Black Elk Speaks*, in which an old Plains Indian man tells how he had a great vision when he was nine years old. He became so sick that everyone thought he was dead. He was in a coma for a week or more, during which he was shown how the sacred way in which his people lived was going to be lost. He was also shown ways to help save it from being completely lost. In this coma he was taken to the top of Harney Peak, in the Black Hills of Dakota, which the Native Americans of the United States regard as the center of the world. But after he had been taken to Harney Peak and been given this great vision, Black Elk said that he realized that everywhere was the center of the world. Basically, everywhere you are is the center of the world. You're always standing in the middle of sacred space, standing in the middle of the circle.

People often say, "Meditation is all very well, but what does it have to do with my life?" What it has to do with your life is that perhaps through this simple practice of paying attention—giving loving-kindness to your speech and your actions and the movements of your mind—you begin to realize that you're always standing in the middle of a sacred circle, and that's your whole life. This room is not the sacred circle. Gampo Abbey is not the sacred circle. Wherever you go for the rest of your life, you're always in the middle of the universe and the circle is always around you. Everyone who walks up to you has entered that sacred space, and it's not an accident. Whatever comes into the space is there to teach you.

Through my experience of Buddhism and my deep love and respect for my teachers, the teachings, and the practices, I've come to see that it's good to stick to one vehicle and go deeper and deeper and deeper. But by doing this, I've begun to see the sacredness of everybody's wisdom and the fact that people discover the same truths through many avenues. Meditation begins to open up your life, so that you're not caught in self-concern, just wanting life to go your way. In that case you no longer realize that you're standing at the center of the world, that you're in the middle of a sacred circle, because you're so concerned with your worries, pains, limitations, desires, and fears that you are blind to the beauty of existence. All you feel by being caught up like this is misery, as well as enormous resentment about life in general. How strange! Life is such a miracle, and a lot of the time we feel only resentment about how it's all working out for us.

There was once a woman who was arrogant and proud. She decided she wanted to attain enlightenment, so she asked all the authorities how to do that. One said, "Well, if you climb to the top of this very high mountain, you'll find a cave there. Sitting inside that cave is a very wise old woman, and she will tell you." So the woman thought, "Good, I'll do that. Nothing but the best." Having endured great hardships, she finally found this cave, and sure enough, sitting there was this very gentle, spiritual-looking old woman in white clothes who smiled at her beatifically. Overcome with awe and respect, she prostrated at the feet of this woman and said, "I want to attain enlightenment. Show me how." The wise woman looked at her with her beatific smile and asked, "Are you sure you want to attain enlightenment?" And the woman said, "Of course I'm sure." Whereupon the smiling woman turned into a demon, stood up brandishing a great big stick, and started chasing her, saying, "Now! Now! Now!" For the rest of her life, that lady could never get away from the demon who was always saying, "Now!"

So often Rinpoche would talk about nowness. The

chapters "Nowness" and "Discovering Magic" in his book *Shambhala: The Sacred Path of the Warrior* are all about what I'm saying here. If you want to attain enlightenment, you have to do it now. If you're arrogant and stubborn, it may take someone running after you with a stick. But the more you open your heart, the more you make friends with your body, speech, mind, and the world that's inside of your circle—your domestic situation, the people you live with, the house you find yourself eating breakfast in every day—the more you appreciate the fact that when you turn on the tap, water comes out. If you have ever lived without water, you really appreciate that. There are all kinds of miracles. Everything is like that, absolutely wonderful.

Now. That's the key. Now, now, now. Mindfulness trains you to be awake and alive, fully curious, about what? Well, about *now,* right? You sit in meditation and the out-breath is now and waking up from your fantasies is now and even the fantasies are now, although they seem to take you into the past and into the future. The more you can be completely *now,* the more you realize that you're in the center of the world, standing in the middle of a sacred circle. It's no small affair, whether you're brushing your teeth or cooking your food or wiping your bottom. Whatever you're doing, you're doing it now.

Our life's work is to use what we have been given to wake up. If there were two people who were exactly the same—same body, same speech, same mind, same mother, same father, same house, same food, everything the same—one of them could use what he has to wake up and the other could use it to become more resentful, bitter, and sour. It doesn't matter what you're given, whether it's physical deformity or enormous wealth or poverty, beauty or ugliness, mental stability or mental instability, life in the middle of a madhouse or life in the middle of a peaceful, silent desert. Whatever you're given can wake you up or put you to sleep. That's the challenge of now: What are you going to do with what you have already—your body, your speech, your mind?

Here's something that's very helpful to know about now. The biggest obstacle to taking a bigger perspective on life is that our emotions capture and blind us. The more sensitive we become to this, the more we realize that when we start getting angry or denigrating ourselves or craving things in a way that makes us feel miserable, we begin to shut down, shut out, as if we were sitting on the edge of the Grand Canyon but we had put a big black bag over our heads.

You can experiment with this. You can go out there to the cliffs overlooking the Gulf of Saint Lawrence, and the first hit is always, "Wow! It's so big," and your mind opens. But if you stand there long enough, you'll start to worry about something. Then you realize (if you want to do this as an exercise) that it feels as if everything is closing down and getting very small.

The trick about nowness is that you can let go and open up again to that space. You can do that at any moment, always. But it does take making friends with yourself. It does take coming to know your anger, coming to know your self-deprecation, coming to know your craving and wanting, coming to know your boredom, and making friends with those things.

There's another story that you may have read that has to do with what we call heaven and hell, life and death, good and bad. It's a story about how those things don't really exist except as a creation of our own minds. It goes like this: A big burly samurai comes to the wise man and says, "Tell me the nature of heaven and hell." And the roshi looks him in the face and says: "Why should I tell a scruffy, disgusting, miserable slob like you?" The samurai starts to get purple in the face, his hair starts to stand up, but the roshi won't stop, he keeps saying, "A miserable worm like you, do you think I should tell you anything?" Consumed by rage, the samurai draws his sword, and he's just about to cut off the head of the roshi. Then the roshi says, "That's hell." The samurai, who is in fact a sensitive person, instantly gets it, that he just created his own hell; he was deep in hell. It was black and hot, filled with hatred, self-protection, anger, and resentment, so much so that he was going to kill this man. Tears fill his eyes and he starts to cry and he puts his palms together and the roshi says, "That's heaven."

There isn't any hell or heaven except for how we relate to our world. Hell is just resistance to life. When you want to say no to the situation you're in, it's fine to say no, but when you build up a big case to the point where you're so convinced that you would draw your sword and cut off someone's head, that kind of resistance to life is hell.

In the way we practice, we don't say, "Hell is bad and heaven is good" or "Get rid of hell and just seek heaven," but we encourage ourselves to develop an open heart and an open mind to heaven, to hell, to everything. Why? Because only then can we realize that no matter what comes along, we're always standing at the center of the world in the middle of sacred space, and everything that comes into that circle and exists with us there has come to teach us what we need to know.

Life's work is to wake up, to let the things that enter into the circle wake you up rather than put you to sleep. The only way to do this is to open, be curious, and develop some sense of sympathy for everything that comes along, to get to know its nature and let it teach you what it will. It's going to stick around until you learn your lesson, at any rate. You can leave your marriage, you can quit your job, you can only go where people are going to praise you, you can manipulate your world until you're blue in the face to try to make it always smooth, but the same old demons will always come up until finally you have learned your lesson, the lesson they came to teach you. Then those same demons will appear as friendly, warm-hearted companions on the path.

So that's why, this morning, even though I was very hungry and tired, I was also very happy. And I would like to express my gratitude to Trungpa Rinpoche for that.

8

No Such Thing as a True Story

IN TAOISM there's a famous saying that goes, "The Tao that can be spoken is not the ultimate Tao." Another way you could say that, although I've never seen it translated this way, is, "As soon as you begin to believe in something, then you can no longer see anything else." The truth you believe in and cling to makes you unavailable to hear anything new.

By the way that we think and by the way that we believe in things, in that way is our world created. In the Middle Ages, everyone accepted the idea, based on fear, that there was only one way to believe; if you didn't believe that way, you were the enemy. It was death to all forms of creative, fresh thinking. Many things that people had been able to see, people just couldn't see anymore because they didn't believe in them. Once they began to think and believe in a certain way, there were all kinds of things that they literally couldn't hear, see, smell, or touch, because those things were outside their belief system.

Holding on to beliefs limits our experience of life. That doesn't mean that beliefs or ideas or thinking is a problem; the stubborn attitude of having to have things be a particular way, grasping on to our beliefs and thoughts, all these cause the problems. To put it simply, using your belief system this way creates a situation in which you choose to be blind instead of being able to see, to be deaf instead of being able to hear, to be dead rather than alive, asleep rather than awake.

Nowadays, some people are stepping out and exploring, but other people are becoming more entrenched in their beliefs. A polarization is occurring, and as a result, for example, we have some Christians getting hysterical about the film *The Last Temptation of Christ* because someone dares to say that Christ is not what a lot of people want to think he is. When a belief system is threatened, people may even become so fanatical that they kill and destroy.

An example is the response of Muslims to Salman Rushdie's novel *Satanic Verses*, in which he suggests that Muhammad was not what they believe he was— and for that they would condemn Rushdie to death. Actually you see this situation everywhere. Protestants are killing Catholics and Catholics are killing Protestants. Hindus are killing Buddhists and Buddhists are killing Hindus. Jews are killing Christians and Christians are killing Jews. Muslims are killing Christians and Christians are killing Muslims. There are wars all over the world because people are insulted that someone else doesn't agree with their belief system.

Everybody is guilty of it. It's what is called fundamental theism. You want something to hold on to, you want to say, "Finally I have found it. This is it, and now I feel confirmed and secure and righteous." Buddhism is not free of it either. This is a human thing. But in Buddhism there is a teaching that would seemingly undercut all this, if people would only listen to it. It says, "If you meet the Buddha on the road, kill the Buddha." This means that if you can find Buddha and say, "It's this way; Buddha is like this," then you had better kill that "Buddha" that you found, that you can say is like this. Contemplative and mystical Christians, Hindus, Jews, people of all faiths and nonfaiths can also have this perspective: if you meet the Christ that can be named, kill that Christ. If you meet the Muhammad, or the Jehovah or whoever that can be named and held on to and believed in, smash it.

Now we get to the interesting part. How do you do that? Although this approach sounds pretty aggressive, when we talk this way, we're actually talking about the ultimate in nonaggression. People find it quite easy to have beliefs and to hold on to them and to let their whole world be a product of their belief system. They also find it quite easy to attack those who disagree. The harder, more courageous thing, which the hero and the heroine, the warrior, and the mystic do, is continually to look one's beliefs straight in the face, honestly and clearly, and then step beyond them. That requires a lot of heart and kindness.

It requires being able to touch and know completely, to the core, your own experience, without harshness, without making any judgment.

"When you meet the Buddha, kill the Buddha" means that when you see that you're grasping or clinging to anything, whether conventionally it's called good or bad, make friends with that. Look into it. Get to know it completely and utterly. In that way it will let go of itself.

It's said in the teachings that if you hold on to your belief there will be conflict. There's a wonderful story about this. There was a god who knew how men and women love to believe things to be true and make clubs and religions and political systems with the people who agree with them. They just love to make something out of nothing and then write its name on a big banner and march down the street waving it and yelling and screaming, only to have people who believe the opposite come toward them with *their* banner, yelling and screaming. This god decided to try to prove a point about the human condition so that people might, in seeing the absurdity of it, have a good laugh. (A good laugh is the best way to kill the Buddha.) He constructed a big hat divided right down the middle, the left side of which was brilliant blue and the right side flaming red. Then he went to a place where many people were working in the fields on the left side of a road and many other people were working in the fields on the right side of the road.

There the god manifested in all his glory; no one could miss him. Big and radiant, wearing his hat, he walked straight down the road. All the people on the right side of the road dropped their hoes and looked up at this god; all the people on the left side of the road did the same. Everybody was amazed. Then he disappeared. Everyone shouted, "We saw God! We saw God!" They were all full of joy, until someone on the left said, "There he was in all his radiance and in his red hat!" And people on the right said, "No, he had on a blue hat." This disagreement escalated until the people built walls and began to throw stones at each other. Then the god appeared again. This time he walked in the other direction and then disappeared. Now all the people looked at each other and the ones on the right said, "Ah, you were right, he did have on a red hat. We're so sorry, we just saw incorrectly. You were right and we were wrong." The ones on the other side said, "No, no. You were right. We were wrong." At this point they didn't know whether to fight or to make friends. Most of them were completely puzzled by the situation. Then the god appeared again. This time he stood in the middle and he turned to the left and then he turned around to the right, and everyone started to laugh.

For us, as people sitting here meditating, as people wanting to live a good, full, unrestricted, adventurous, real kind of life, there is concrete instruction that we can follow, which is the one that we have been following all along in meditation: see what is. Acknowledge it without judging it as right or wrong. Let it go and come back to the present moment. Whatever comes up, see what is without calling it right or wrong. Acknowledge it. See it clearly without judgment and let it go. Come back to the present moment. From now until the moment of your death, you could do this. As a way of becoming more compassionate toward yourself and toward others, as a way of becoming less dogmatic, prejudiced, determined to have your own way, absolutely sure that you're right and the other person is wrong, as a way to develop a sense of humor about the whole thing, to lighten it up, open it up, you could do this. You could also begin to notice whenever you find yourself blaming others or justifying yourself. If you spent the rest of your life just noticing that and letting it be a way to uncover the silliness of the human condition—the tragic yet comic drama that we all continually buy into—you could develop a lot of wisdom and a lot of kindness as well as a great sense of humor.

Seeing when you justify yourself and when you blame others is not a reason to criticize yourself, but actually an opportunity to recognize what all people do and how it imprisons us in a very limited perspective of this world. It's a chance to see that you're holding on to your interpretation of reality; it allows you to reflect that that's all it is—nothing more, nothing less; just your interpretation of reality.

9

Weather and the Four Noble Truths

WHEN THE BUDDHA first taught, he could have taught anything. He had just waked up completely. His mind was clear and he experienced no obstacles—just the vastness and goodness of himself and his life. The story goes, however, that it was difficult for him to express his experience; initially he decided not to teach because he thought no one would be able to understand what he was talking about. He finally decided that he *would* go out and he *would* teach because there were some people who would hear him. The interesting thing is that at first he didn't talk about the unconditional; he didn't talk about basic goodness, clarity, space, bliss, wonder, or openness. In the first teaching of the Buddha—the teachings on the four noble truths—he talked about suffering.

I've always experienced these teachings as a tremendous affirmation that there is no need to resist being fully alive in this world, that we are in fact part of the web. All of life is interconnected. If something lives, it has life force, the quality of which is energy, a sense of spiritedness. Without that, we can't lift our arms or open our mouths or open and shut our eyes. If you have ever been with someone who is dying, you know that at one moment, even though it might be quite weak, there's life force there, and then the next moment there is none. It's said that when we die, the four elements—earth, air, fire, water—dissolve one by one, each into the other, and finally just dissolve into space. But while we're living, we share the energy that makes everything, from a blade of grass to an elephant, grow and live and then inevitably wear out and die. This energy, this life force, creates the whole world. It's very curious that because we as human beings have consciousness, we are also subject to a little twist where we resist life's energies.

I was talking to a man the other day who has severe depression. When he gets depressed, he sits in a chair; he can't move. All he does is worry. He said that all winter long he sat in the chair, thinking that he ought to go bring the lawn mower out of the snow, but he just couldn't do it. Now that's not what I mean by sitting still. Sitting still, or holding one's seat, means not being pulled away from being fully right there, fully acknowledging and experiencing your life energy. So what happens? I can tell you my experience of it. I was sitting, doing the technique, when this bad feeling came along. Next thing I knew, I was thinking all kinds of things, worrying about something that's going to happen in September, worrying about who is going to take care of the minutest little details of something that's going to happen in October. Then I remembered: sitting still in the middle of a fire or a tornado or an earthquake or a tidal wave, sitting still. This provides the opportunity to experience once again the living quality of our life's energy—earth, air, fire, and water.

Why do we resist our energy? Why do we resist the life force that flows through us? The first noble truth says that if you are alive, if you have a heart, if you can love, if you can be compassionate, if you can realize the life energy that makes everything change and move and grow and die, then you won't have any resentment or resistance. The first noble truth says simply that it's part of being human to feel discomfort. We don't even have to call it suffering anymore, we don't even have to call it discomfort. It's simply coming to know the fieriness of fire, the wildness of wind, the turbulence of water, the upheaval of earth, as well as the warmth of fire, the coolness and smoothness of water, the gentleness of the breezes, and the goodness, solidity, and dependability of the earth. Nothing in its essence is one way or the other. The four elements take on different qualities; they're like magicians. Sometimes they manifest in one form and sometimes in another. If we feel that that's a problem, we resist it. The first noble truth recognizes that we also change like the weather, we ebb and flow like the tides, we wax and wane like the moon. *We* do that, and there's no reason to resist it. If we resist it, the reality and vitality of life become misery, a hell.

The second noble truth says that this resistance is the fundamental operating mechanism of what we call ego, that resisting life causes suffering. Traditionally it's said that the cause of suffering is clinging to our narrow view. Another way to say the same thing is that resisting our complete unity with all of life, resisting the fact that we change and flow like the weather, that we have the same energy as all living things, resisting that is what's called ego.

Yesterday I began to be very curious about the experience of resistance. I noticed that I was sitting there with uncomfortable feelings in my heart and my stomach—dread, you could call it. I began to recognize the opportunity of experiencing the realness of the four elements, feeling what it's like to be weather. Of course that didn't make the discomfort go away, but it removed the resistance, and somehow the world was there again. When I didn't resist, I could see the world. Then I noticed that I had never liked the quality of this particular "weather" for some reason and so I resisted it. In doing that, I realized, I re-created myself. It's as if, when you resist, you dig in your heels. It's as if you're a block of marble and you carve yourself out of it, you make yourself really solid. In my case, worrying about things that are going to happen is very unpleasant; it's an addiction.

It's also unpleasant to get drunk again if you're an alcoholic, or to have to keep shooting up if you're a drug addict, or to keep eating if you have overeating addiction, or whatever it is. All these things are very strange. We all know what addiction is; we are primarily addicted to ME.

Interestingly enough, when the weather changes and the energy simply flows through us, just as it flows through the grass and the trees and the ravens and the bears and the moose and the ocean and the rocks, we discover that we are not solid at all. If we sit still, like the mountain Gampo Lhatse in a hurricane, if we don't protect ourselves from the trueness and the vividness and the immediacy and the lack of confirmation of simply being part of life, then we are not this separate being who has to have things turn out our way.

The third noble truth says that the cessation of suffering is letting go of holding on to ourselves. By "cessation" we mean the cessation of hell as opposed to just weather, the cessation of this resistance, this resentment, this feeling of being completely trapped and caught, trying to maintain huge ME at any cost. The teachings about recognizing egolessness sound quite abstract, but the path quality of that, the magic instruction that we have all received, the golden key is that part of the meditation technique where you recognize what's happening with you and you say to yourself, "Thinking." Then you let go of all the talking and the fabrication and the discussion, and you're left just sitting with the weather—the quality and the energy of the weather itself. Maybe you still have that quaky feeling or that churning feeling or that exploding feeling or that calm feeling or that dull feeling, as if you'd just been buried in the earth. You're left with that. That's the key: come to know *that*. The only way you can know that is by realizing that you've been talking about it, turning it into worry about next week and next October and the rest of your life. It's as if, curiously enough, instead of sitting still in the middle of the fire, we have developed this self-created device for fanning it, keeping it going. Fan that fire, fan that fire. "Well, what about if I don't do this, then that will happen, and if that happens then this will happen, maybe I better get rid of such-and-such and get this and do that. I better tell so-and-so about this, and if I don't tell them that, surely the whole thing is going to fall apart, and then what will happen? Oh, I think I want to die and I want to get out of here. This is horrible and—" Suddenly you want to jump out of your seat and go screaming out of the room. You've been fanning the fire. But at some point you think, "Wait a minute. Thinking." Then you let go and come back to that original fluttering feeling that might be very edgy but is basically the wind, the fire, the earth, the water. I'm not talking about turning a hurricane into a calm day. I'm talking about realizing hurricane-ness, or, if it's a calm day, calmness. I'm not talking about turning a forest fire into a cozy fire in the fireplace or something that's under your cooking pot that heats your stew. I'm saying that when there's a forest fire, don't resist that kind of power—that's you. When it's warm and cozy, don't resist that or nest in it. I'm not saying turn an earthquake into a garden of flowers. When there's an earthquake, let the ground tremble and rip apart, and when it's a rich garden with flowers, let that be also. I'm talking about not resisting, not grasping, not getting caught in hope and in fear, in good and in bad, but actually living completely.

The essence of the fourth noble truth is the eightfold path. Everything we do—our discipline, effort, meditation, livelihood, and every single thing that we do from the moment we're born until the moment we die—we can use to help us to realize our unity and our completeness with all things. We can use our lives, in other words, to wake up to the fact that we're not separate: the energy that causes us to live and be whole and awake and alive is just the energy that creates everything, and we're part of that. We can use our lives to connect with that, or we can use them to become resentful, alienated, resistant, angry, bitter. As always, it's up to us.

10

Not Too Tight, Not Too Loose

TODAY WE WILL talk about how to find one's balance in life. When all is said and done, what in the world is the middle way?

My middle way and your middle way are not the same middle way. For instance, my style is to be casual and soft-edged and laid-back. For me to do what usually would be called strict practice is still pretty relaxed, because I do it in a relaxed way. So strict practice is good for me. It helps me find my middle way. Very relaxed practice doesn't show me as much because it doesn't show me where I'm out of balance. But perhaps you are much more militant and precise and on the dot. Maybe you tend toward being tight. It might be easy for you to do tight practice, but that might be too harsh and too authoritarian, so you might need to find out what it means to practice in a relaxed, loose way. Everybody is different. Everybody's middle way is a different middle way; everyone practices in order to find out for him- or herself personally how to be balanced, how to be not too tight and not too loose. No one else can tell you. You just have to find out for yourself.

In a poem in *First Thought, Best Thought*, Trungpa

Rinpoche says something like, "Buddhism doesn't tell you what is false and what is true, but it encourages you to find out for yourself." Learning to be not too tight and not too loose is an individual journey through which you discover how to find your own balance: how to relax when you find yourself being too rigid; how to become more elegant and precise when you find yourself being too casual.

It seems that it is a common experience to take extreme views; we don't usually find the middle view. For example, we come to a dathun and we're all just starting to practice. The first couple of days we think, "I am going to do this perfectly," and we practice with intense effort to sit right, walk right, breathe right, keep the silence, do everything. We really push; we have a project. Then, at a certain point, we say, "Oh, for goodness' sake! What in the world am I doing?" We may just drop the whole thing and go to the other extreme—"I couldn't care less." The humor and the beauty of practice is that going from one extreme to another is not considered to be an obstacle; sometimes we're like a drill sergeant, sometimes we're like mashed potatoes. Basically, once we have some sort of joyful curiosity about the whole thing, it's simply all information, gathering the information we need to find our own balance.

You're sitting there and all of a sudden you see yourself as a South American dictator and you think, "This is ridiculous." You remember all the instructions about lightening up, softening up, and being more gentle. Then some humor or insight, some sort of gentleness comes in. Another time you are sitting there looking at your fingernails, scratching your ears, fooling with your toes, discovering the inside of your nose and the backs of your ears, and you can see Gary Larson doing a nice little cartoon drawing of yourself. You think, "Well, you know, I could just be a little more precise here." Humor is a much more effective approach than taking your practice in a grimly serious way.

In 1979, at the Vajradhatu Seminary,* Trungpa Rinpoche gave some extremely precise and brilliant teachings that were encouraging to everybody. For years we had received the straight teachings on *shamatha* (mindfulness) practice; these new teachings—the nine different ways of resting the mind—made that practice clearer and more precise because they gave us more sense of how to proceed. The basic idea in these teachings is to find your own balance between being not too tight and not too loose. I'll go through them now; they are very helpful.

First of all, don't regard these nine ways as linear, even though the last one seems to have more of a fruition quality than some of the others. They are not considered to be steps one through nine, but simply nine different suggestions, nine different helpful

---

*A three-month-long program for qualified students interested in pursuing systematic training in the three yanas, or "vehicles" (hinayana, mahayana, and vajrayana) of Tibetan Buddhism.

hints on how to rest your mind in its natural state—how to keep your mind from going to one extreme or another. You could say these are instructions on how to find out what *is* the natural state. What is balance? What is a sense of equanimity? We'd all like to know that. The basic guideline is to see what's too tight for you and what's too loose for you, and you'll discover it. Rather than trying to rest in the middle, just see what's too tight and see what's too loose, and then you'll find your own middle way.

These nine ways have funny names; they all sound the same with a little bit of difference. The first one is called resting, the second one is called continuously resting, the third one is called naively resting, the fourth one is called thoroughly resting, and so on.

The first one is "resting the mind." We've already been instructed to "be one-pointedly with the breath." Even though there are colors and sounds and other people, even though your ears and your nose and your mouth and your tactile senses still exist and none of them goes away, nevertheless, when you sit down to practice, you somehow limit your awareness to the breath as it goes out. Perhaps "limit" is not the right word. You put the main part of your attention, the main part of your mindfulness, onto the breath as it goes out. At the beginning of each session, there's some sense of simplifying down to just that breath. The instruction is *not* "Blot out all the other things." There's still just that twenty-five percent awareness.

Nevertheless, it's very important that each time you start, you have some sense of remembering what you're doing: you simplify your main awareness onto the breath. You are quite one-pointed that way. You can do this anytime during your sitting period. You may get all caught up during the session, and then you can just stop, rest, and start again, a fresh start. Always start with that sense of the main emphasis being on the breath.

In the second instruction, "continually resting," you are encouraged to prolong that sense of being fully with the breath. Sometimes it could be sort of a one-shot deal, and then the rest could be softer. But sometimes it happens naturally that you can elongate that sense of feeling the breath as it goes out, that sense of being fully with the breath. The instruction for continuously resting is to train yourself not to be distracted by every little thing, but to stay with the breath. So the first instruction is something you can do, and the second one is something that tends to be an attitude and an experience that evolves: you are not drawn off by every sound, not distracted by every sight, not completely captured by every movement of your mind. You are able to prolong that sense of sitting in the present moment, being fully there, just breathing.

The third one is "naively resting," sometimes called "literally resting." This instruction has to do with taking a naive attitude, a childlike attitude toward your practice, keeping it very simple. It's about not getting conceptual and intellectual about the shamatha-vipashyana instruction. It says: when your mind wanders off, without making any big deal whatsoever, simply come back. Usually we don't just simply come back. Either we don't even notice that we're thinking and then we come back, or we're very militant and judgmental. So naively resting says, "Just simply come back." When Trungpa Rinpoche talks about this, he uses the example of feeding a baby. You're trying to get the spoon into the baby's mouth, and the baby's attention is wandering all over the place. You just say, "See the birdy," and the baby's attention comes back, and you stick the spoon in the baby's mouth. It's very simple. The baby doesn't say, "Oh, bad baby! I was thinking." The baby just says "Food!" and comes back. I can give you another example. You're brushing your teeth and your attention wanders off. All of a sudden you realize that you're standing there with toothpaste frothing in your mouth, yet you've just taken a quick trip to Los Angeles. You simply come back to brushing your teeth; there's no sense of big deal. That's naively resting.

The fourth of the nine ways, is "thoroughly resting." The instruction here is to let yourself settle down, let your mind calm down. If you then find there are no 3-D movies going on, then try to catch each flicker of thought, the tiniest flickers of thought. The example given is that sometimes your thought is like a little flea touching you on the nose and jumping off, whereas other times it's like an elephant sitting on you. The instruction is that you could try to catch just the tiny flickers of thought. In your practice, you'll know when you are feeling settled like that and when you could try practicing that way. You'll also sometimes find that it just comes to you and that's how it is.

The fifth one is called "taming the mind." This has to do with the importance of a basic attitude of friendliness. Sometimes when our thoughts are like little fleas that jump off our noses, we just see the little flickers of thought, like ripples, which might have a very liberating quality. For the first time you might feel, "My goodness! There's so much space, and it's always been here." Another time it might feel like that elephant is sitting on you, or like you have your own private pornographic movie going on, or your own private war, in technicolor and stereo. It's important to realize that meditation doesn't prefer the flea to the elephant, or vice versa. It is simply a process of seeing what is, noticing that, accepting that, and then going on with life, which, in terms of the technique, is coming back to the simplicity of nowness, the simplicity of the out-breath. Whether you are completely caught up in discursive thought for the entire sitting period, or whether you feel that enormous sense of space, you can regard either one with gentleness and a sense of being awake and alive to who you are. Either way, you can respect that. So taming teaches that meditation is developing a nonaggressive attitude to whatever occurs in your mind. It teaches that meditation is not considering yourself an obstacle to yourself; in fact, it's quite the opposite.

Number six, "pacifying," is further instruction on how to deal with negativity. Taming basically gave the view, which is so crucial, that meditation is cultivating nonaggression and a good relationship with ourselves. Pacifying acknowledges that when we've really committed ourselves to practice, when we have some passion for practice and we put our whole self into it, a very curious thing always happens: we get fed up, we lose heart, and we get discouraged. We might say, "I don't want to do this," and just long to put on our backpack and hike down to the end of the point, or get into a boat and sail out to sea, or have longer breaks and more to eat, and "Let's get a good night's sleep for once!" Pacifying is a teaching with a lot of good humor in it. It recognizes what it's like for all of us (and apparently, since these teachings are over two thousand years old, it's always been like this). It says, "First of all, recognize that a letdown feeling accompanies good practice, that this is the experience of someone who is very committed and has started on a journey, and pacify yourself. When that happens, see that there's some humor in it, and just talk to yourself, encourage yourself." You can say things like, "Oh! Here it comes again. I thought I had gotten rid of this one, but here it is. Oh, my goodness! I had never experienced this, but this is just what she was talking about." You can actually talk to yourself about how precious our human life is and how uncertain the length of it is, and realize that it's a rare and precious opportunity to be able to make friends with yourself so completely and thoroughly. You can sit down in silence with yourself and simply see who you are and, in a gentle and precise way, continually be with yourself, learning how to acknowledge fully who you are and to let go of the tendency to fixate and dwell. So pacifying is realizing the human condition with a lot of heart and a lot of sympathy, and appreciating the rareness and preciousness of being able to practice and make friends with yourself. You can also realize that, at a time like this, when there's so much chaos and crisis and suffering in the world, we are actually needed. Individuals who are willing to wake up and make friends with themselves are going to be very beneficial, because they can work with others, they can hear what people are saying to them, and they can come from the heart and be of use. So you can encourage yourself in that way, which is called pacifying.

"Thoroughly pacifying," number seven, gives specific instructions about the obstacles and antidotes. It talks about passion, aggression, and ignorance, which we consider to be obstacles to practice. It says that if you are experiencing extreme aggression in your practice, first you can take that sense of fresh start, and then you can emphasize the airy, windy, fresh quality of your breath. You have learned the meditation technique, you have posture and labeling and all kinds of tools, but if aggression has its claws in you and you can't let go of those resentful, bitter, angry thoughts and plans, then you should emphasize the windy, airy, fresh quality of the breath as it goes out, which helps you connect with freshness and spaciousness.

If it's passion or lust that has taken hold of you—you can't stop thinking about that person or that thing that you want so much—then the instruction, interestingly enough, is to flash back to your sense of body, emphasize your posture. The antidote to being completely caught by lust and passion, wanting so much that it hurts, is your posture. Just resettle and have this sense of mindfulness of body. Just emphasize feeling your hands on your thighs and feeling your bottom on the cushion. You could even mentally go through your whole body from the top of your head all the way down. Come into your body completely to ground yourself.

The antidote for ignorance or drowsiness is connecting with spaciousness, the opposite of the antidote for passion, which is connecting with sense of body. If ignorance of drowsiness is a problem, then you can sense your breath dissolving into space; you can sense your body sitting in this room with all this space around you, all the space outside the abbey and all the space of the whole of Cape Breton Island: lots of space. You connect with a sense of big space to wake yourself up, brighten things up. Rather than having your eyes somewhat lowered, you can raise your gaze, but without starting to look around.

Number eight, "one-pointedness," has two parts, with the main emphasis on this notion of fresh start. If your mind is all caught up and driving you crazy, you can just stop practicing altogether. Just stop practicing. Give up the whole struggle. Give yourself a break. For a while, don't practice. Keep your posture, so you don't become too loose, but on the other hand let your mind relax and just think about things or look out. Relax, and then start fresh. The second part of this particular teaching is realizing that you're not a victim of anything, and neither are you a patient that some doctor has to cure. You're actually a sane, healthy, decent, basically good person, and you can find your own balance. This sense of fresh start can be applied not only to formal meditation, but throughout your whole life. This teaching, one-pointedness, means that you can be thoroughly present. If you find yourself feeling distracted, you can simply come back and wake up and give yourself a fresh start. There are ways of doing what you want to do and ways of being who you want to be. You don't have to feel like a victim of your own mind.

The last of the nine ways is called "resting evenly." It is also sometimes called absorption. However, Rinpoche made it very clear that this is not some kind of absorption state that blocks everything else out. Resting evenly just stresses the basic attitude that meditation is about developing a thoroughly good friendship with oneself, a completely honest, openhearted relationship with oneself. Traditionally there's a little verse that goes with this teaching, which says, "As swans swim on the lake and vultures roam in the charnel ground, you can let your mind rest in its natural state."

II

Renunciation

WHEN PEOPLE take refuge in the formal ceremony of becoming a Buddhist, they receive a name that indicates their main path, how they should work, their main vehicle. I've noticed that when people get the name "Renunciation," they hate it. It makes them feel terrible; they feel as if someone gave them the name "Torture Chamber," or perhaps "Torture Chamber of Enlightenment." People usually don't like the name "Discipline" either. But so much depends on how you look at these things. Renunciation does not have to be regarded as negative. I was taught that it has to do with letting go of holding back. What one is renouncing is closing down and shutting off from life. You could say that renunciation is the same thing as opening to the teachings of the present moment.

It's probably good to think of the ground of renunciation as being our good old selves, our basic decency and sense of humor. In Buddhist teachings and in the Shambhala teachings, as well as in the teachings of many other contemplative or mystical traditions, the basic view is that people are fundamentally good and healthy. It's as if everyone who has ever been born has the same birthright, which is enormous potential of warm heart and clear mind. The ground of renunciation is realizing that we already have exactly what we need, that what we have already is good. Every moment of time has enormous energy in it, and we could connect with that.

I was recently in a doctor's office that had a poster on the wall of an old Native American woman walking along a road, holding the hand of a little child. The caption read: "The seasons come and go, summer follows spring and fall follows summer and winter follows fall, and human beings are born and mature, have their middle age, begin to grow older and die, and everything has its cycles. Day follows night, night follows day. It is good to be part of all of this." When you begin to have that kind of trust in basic creativity and directness and fullness, in the alive quality of yourself and your world, then you can begin to understand renunciation.

Trungpa Rinpoche once said, "Renunciation is realizing that nostalgia for samsara* is full of shit." Renunciation is realizing that our nostalgia for wanting to stay in a protected, limited, petty world is insane. Once you begin to get the feeling of how big the world is and how vast our potential for experiencing

---

*The vicious cycle of existence—the round of birth and death and rebirth—which arises out of ignorance and is characterized by suffering; in ordinary reality, the vicious cycle of frustration and suffering generated as the result of karma (one's actions).

life is, then you really begin to understand renunciation. When we sit in meditation, we feel our breath
as it goes out, and we have some sense of willingness
just to be open to the present moment. Then our
minds wander off into all kinds of stories and fab-
rications and manufactured realities, and we say to
ourselves, "It's thinking." We say that with a lot of
gentleness and a lot of precision. Every time we are
willing to let the story line go, and every time we are
willing to let go at the end of the out-breath, that's
fundamentally renunciation: learning how to let go
of holding on and holding back.

The river flows rapidly down the mountain, and
then all of a sudden it gets blocked with big boulders
and a lot of trees. The water can't go any farther, even
though it has tremendous force and forward energy. It
just gets blocked there. That's what happens with us
too; we get blocked like that. Letting go at the end of
the out-breath, letting the thoughts go, is like moving
one of those boulders away so that the water can keep
flowing, so that our energy and our life force can keep
evolving and going forward. We don't, out of fear of
the unknown, have to put up these blocks, these
dams, that basically say no to life and to feeling life.

So renunciation is seeing clearly how we hold
back, how we pull away, how we shut down, how we
close off, and then learning how to open. It's about
saying yes to whatever is put on your plate, whatever
knocks on your door, whatever calls you up on your

telephone. How we actually do that has to do with coming up against our edge, which is actually the moment when we learn what renunciation means. There is a story about a group of people climbing to the top of a mountain. It turns out it's pretty steep, and as soon as they get up to a certain height, a couple of people look down and see how far it is, and they completely freeze; they had come up against their edge and they couldn't go beyond it. The fear was so great that they couldn't move. Other people tripped on ahead, laughing and talking, but as the climb got steeper and more scary, more people began to get scared and freeze. All the way up this mountain there were places where people met their edge and just froze and couldn't go any farther. The people who made it to the top looked out and were very happy to have made it to the top. The moral of the story is that it really doesn't make any difference where you meet your edge; just meeting it is the point. Life is a whole journey of meeting your edge again and again. That's where you're challenged; that's where, if you're a person who wants to live, you start to ask yourself questions like, "Now, why am I so scared? What is it that I don't want to see? Why can't I go any further than this?" The people who got to the top were not the heroes of the day. It's just that they weren't afraid of heights; they are going to meet their edge somewhere else. The ones who froze at the bottom were not the losers. They simply stopped first and so their lesson came earlier than the others. However, sooner or later everybody meets his or her edge.

When we meditate, we're creating a situation in which there's a lot of space. That sounds good but actually it can be unnerving, because when there's a lot of space you can see very clearly: you've removed your veils, your shields, your armor, your dark glasses, your earplugs, your layers and layers of mittens, your heavy boots. Finally you're standing, touching the earth, feeling the sun on your body, feeling its brightness, hearing all the noises without anything to dull the sound. You take off your nose plug, and maybe you're going to smell lovely fresh air or maybe you're in the middle of a garbage dump or a cesspool. Since meditation has this quality of bringing you very close to yourself and your experience, you tend to come up against your edge faster. It's not an edge that wasn't there before, but because things are so simplified and clear, you see it, and you see it vividly and clearly.

How do we renounce? How do we work with this tendency to block and to freeze and to refuse to take another step toward the unknown? If our edge is like a huge stone wall with a door in it, how do we learn to open that door and step through it again and again, so that life becomes a process of growing up, becoming more and more fearless and flexible, more and more able to play like a raven in the wind?

The wilder the weather is, the more the ravens love it. They have the time of their lives in the winter, when the wind gets much stronger and there's lots of ice and snow. They challenge the wind. They get up on the tops of the trees and they hold on with their claws and then they grab on with their beaks as well. At some point they just let go into the wind and let it blow them away. Then they play on it, they float on it. After a while, they'll go back to the tree and start over. It's a game. Once I saw them in an incredible hurricane-velocity wind, grabbing each other's feet and dropping and then letting go and flying out. It was like a circus act. The animals and the plants here on Cape Breton are hardy and fearless and playful and joyful; the elements have strengthened them. In order to exist here, they have had to develop a zest for challenge and for life. As you can see, it adds up to tremendous beauty and inspiration and uplifted feeling. The same goes for us.

If we understand renunciation properly, we also will serve as an inspiration for other people because of our hero quality, our warrior quality, the fact that each of us meets our challenges all the time. When somebody works with hardship in an openhearted humorous way like a warrior, when somebody cultivates his or her bravery, everyone responds, because we know *we* can do that too. We know that this person wasn't born perfect but was inspired to cultivate warriorship and a gentle heart and clarity.

Whenever you realize you have met your edge— you're scared and you're frozen and you're blocked— you're able to recognize it because you open enough to see what's happening. It's already a sign of your aliveness and the fact that you've shed a lot, that you can see so clearly and so vividly. Rather than think you have made a mistake, you can acknowledge the present moment and its teaching, or so we are instructed. You can hear the message, which is simply that you're saying "No." The instruction isn't then to "smash ahead and karate-chop that whole thing"; the instruction is to soften, to connect with your heart and engender a basic attitude of generosity and compassion toward yourself, the archetypal coward.

The journey of awakening—the classical journey of the mythical hero or heroine—is one of continually coming up against big challenges and then learning how to soften and open. In other words, the paralyzed quality seems to be hardening and refusing, and the letting go or the renunciation of that attitude is simply feeling the whole thing in your heart, letting it touch your heart. You soften and feel compassion for your predicament and for the whole human condition. You soften so that you can actually sit there with those troubling feelings and let them soften you more.

The whole journey of renunciation, or starting to say yes to life, is first of all realizing that you've come up against your edge, that everything in you is saying no, and then at that point, softening. This is yet another opportunity to develop loving-kindness for yourself, which results in playfulness—learning to play like a raven in the wind.

12

Sending and Taking

THIS MORNING I'm going to talk about *tonglen*, the practice of "sending and taking." Some of you have done it before and some of you haven't, but in any case, it's always like doing it for the first time.

Tonglen practice has to do with cultivating fearlessness. When you do this practice for some time, you experience your heart as more open. You begin to realize that fear has to do with wanting to protect your heart: you feel that something is going to harm your heart, and therefore you protect it. Again and again, in the Buddhist teachings, in the Shambhala teachings, and in any tradition that teaches us how to live well, we are encouraged to cultivate fearlessness. How do we do that? Certainly the sitting practice of meditation is one way, because through it we come to know ourselves so completely and with such gentleness.

I had been doing shamatha practice for maybe seven years when I first did tonglen. After doing this practice, I was amazed to see how I had been subtly using my shamatha to try to avoid being hurt, to try to avoid depression or discouragement or bad feelings of any kind. Basically, unknown to myself, I had secretly hoped that if I did the practice I wouldn't have to feel any pain anymore. When you do tonglen, you invite the pain in. That's what opens your eyes, even though that's what shamatha is all about—seeing pain, seeing pleasure, seeing everything with gentleness and accuracy, without judging it, without pushing it away, becoming more open to it. Even though that's what we've been practicing all along, tonglen puts it right on the line; I realized that I hadn't really been doing that before. Tonglen takes a lot of courage to do. Interestingly enough, it also gives you a lot of courage. You start out maybe with one thimbleful of courage and a tremendous aspiration to want to open to your world and to be of benefit to yourself and others. You know that that means you're going to find yourself in places where all your buttons will be pushed and things are going to be tough, but nevertheless, you have the aspiration to be able to walk into any situation and be of benefit. You have at the most only a thimbleful of courage, just enough courage to do tonglen, maybe because you don't known what you're getting into, but that's usually life's situation anyway! Something amazing then occurs. By the willingness to do tonglen, you find, after some time—a few days or a few months or a few years—that you have a teacup full of courage, that somehow, by doing the practice, you awaken your heart and you awaken your courage. When I say "awaken your heart," I mean that you're willing not to cover over the most tender part of yourself. Trungpa Rinpoche often talked about the fact that we all have a soft spot and that negativity and resentment and all those things occur because we're trying to cover over our soft spot. That's very positive logic: it's because you are tender and deeply touched that you do all this shielding. It's because you're soft and have some kind of warm heart, an open quality, to begin with that you even start shielding.

In shamatha particularly, you see your shields so clearly. You see how you imprison your heart. That already lightens things up and gives you some respect for the insight and perhaps sense of humor that you have. Tonglen takes that further because you actually invite in not only all your own unresolved conflicts, confusion, and pain, but also those of other people. And it goes even further. Usually we try to ward off feeling bad, and when we feel good we would like that to last forever. In tonglen, though, not only are we willing to breathe in painful things, we are also willing to breathe out our feelings of well-being, peace, and joy. We are willing to give these away, to share them with others. Tonglen is quite the opposite of the conventional approach. Usually if one is meditating and one really begins to connect with something bigger and feel the sense of inspiration and delight, even walking meditation seems like an intrusion. Having to clean the toilet and talk with people definitely seems to get in the way of our bliss. The tonglen approach is, "If you feel it, share it. Don't hold on to it. Give it away."

Mahayana* Buddhism talks about *bodhicitta*, which means "awakened heart" or "courageous heart." Bodhicitta has the qualities of gentleness, precision, and openness, being able just to let go and open up. Specifically, the purpose of tonglen is to awaken or cultivate bodhicitta, to awaken your heart or cultivate your courageous heart. It's like watering a seed that can flower. You might feel that you have only that little thimbleful of courage, or you might feel that you don't have any courage at all, but the Buddha said, "Hogwash! Everyone has bodhicitta." So maybe it's just a little sesame seed of bodhicitta, but if you do the practice, it's like watering that seed, which seems to grow and flourish. What's really happening is that what was there all along is being uncovered. Doing tonglen sweeps away the dust that has been covering over your treasure that's always been there.

Traditionally, bodhicitta is compared to a diamond that's been covered over with ten tons of mud for two thousand years. You could uncover it at any point and it would still be a jewel, our heirloom. Bodhicitta is also said to be like very rich, creamy milk that has the potential of being butter. You have to do a little work to get the butterness out of the cream. You have to churn it. It's also been compared to a sesame seed, full of sesame oil. You have to do a little pounding to

---

*The "great vehicle," which presents vision based on emptiness, compassion, and acknowledgment of universal buddha nature.

get the oil, but it's already there. Sometimes bodhicitta is said to be like a precious treasure lying at the
side of the road with a few dirty rags over it. People—
perhaps very poor people who are starving to death—
walk by it all the time. All they have to do is just pick
up the rags, and there it is. We do tonglen so that we
don't have to be like blind people, continually walking over this jewel that's right there. We don't have to
feel like poverty-stricken paupers, because right in
our heart is everything anyone could ever wish for
in terms of open, courageous warmth and clarity.
Everybody has it, but not everybody has the courage
to let it ripen.

These days the world really needs people who
are willing to let their hearts, their bodhicitta, ripen.
There's such widespread devastation and suffering:
people are being run over by tanks or their houses are
being blown up or soldiers are knocking on their
doors in the middle of the night and taking them
away and torturing them and killing their children
and their loved ones. People are starving. It's a hard
time. We who are living in the lap of luxury with our
pitiful little psychological problems have a tremendous responsibility to let our clarity and our heart,
our warmth, and our ability ripen, to open up and let
go, because it's so contagious. Have you noticed that
if you walk into the dining room and sit down and the
one other person who is there is feeling good and you
know he's feeling good, somehow it includes you, it

makes you feel good, as if he liked you? But if you go
into the dining room and the one other person who's
there is feeling really crummy, you wonder, "What
did I do?" or "Gosh, I better do something to try to
make him feel good." Whether you're having a headache or an attack of depression or whatever is happening with you, if you feel at home in your world,
it's contagious; it could give other people a break. We
can give each other this break by being willing to
work with our own fear and our own feelings of inad-
equacy and our own early-morning depression and
all of that.

Practicing shamatha is one way of showing your
willingness to see things clearly and without judging.
Doing tonglen is a gesture toward ripening your bodhicitta for the sake of your own happiness and that
of others. Your own happiness radiates out, giving
others the space to connect with their own joy, intelligence, clarity, and warmth.

The essence of tonglen practice is that on the in-
breath you are willing to feel pain: you're willing to
acknowledge the suffering of the world. From this
day onward, you're going to cultivate your bravery
and willingness to feel that part of the human condition. You breathe in so that you can really understand
what the Buddha meant when he said that the first
noble truth is that life is suffering. What does that
mean? With every in-breath, you try to find out by
acknowledging the truth of suffering, not as a mis-

take you made, not as a punishment, but as part of the human condition. With every in-breath, you explore the discomfort of the human condition, which can be acknowledged and celebrated and not run away from. Tonglen puts it right on the line.

The essence of the out-breath is the other part of the human condition. With every out-breath, you open. You connect with the feeling of joy, well-being, satisfaction, tenderheartedness, anything that feels fresh and clean, wholesome and good. That's the aspect of the human condition that we wish were the whole show, the part that, if we could finally clear up all our problems, we would have as our everyday diet. The menu would read, "Only happiness. No pain here." There would be all the things that you think would bring you everlasting happiness, maybe a little bittersweetness, a few little tears, but definitely no heavy-duty confusion, no dark places, no closet doors that you don't want to open, no monsters under the bed, no ugly thoughts, no rage, no despair, no jealousy—definitely not. That's the out-breath, the part you like. You connect with that and you breathe it out so that it spreads and can be experienced by everyone.

All that you need in order to do tonglen is to have experienced suffering and to have experienced happiness. Even if you've had only one second of suffering in your life, you can do tonglen. Even if you've had only one second of happiness, you can do tonglen. Those are the prerequisites. In other words,

you are an ordinary human being with pain and pleasure, just like everyone else. However, if you were
just like everyone else, you would breathe in the good
part and breathe out the bad part. Sometimes that
makes a certain amount of sense. But this path, the
path of the warrior, is a lot more daring: you are cultivating a fearless heart, a heart that doesn't close
down in any circumstance; it is always totally open,
so that you could be touched by anything.

There is a classic painting of the wheel of life with
Yama, the god of death, holding the wheel. In the
center is passion, a cock; aggression, a snake; and ignorance, a pig. The spokes of the wheel make six pie-
shaped spaces that are called the six realms. The
lower realms are the hell realm, the hungry ghost
realm (also a very painful one), and the animal realm,
which is full of fear and ignorance, since in that realm
you are able to relate only to what is in front of your
nose. The higher realms are the human realm, the
jealous god realm, and the god realm. In each of those
six realms stands the Buddha, which is to say, we ourselves. We can open our hearts to the point that we
could enter into the hell realm, the hungry ghost
realm, the jealous god realm, the god realm—any
place. We could be there with our hearts, completely
open and not afraid. That's the aspiration of the bodhisattva. When we formally take the bodhisattva
vow, we are given the tonglen practice to do. That
means that we really wish to be fearless enough to

help others; we are aware that we ourselves have a lot of fear, but we aspire to have our hearts wake up completely.

Breathing in, breathing out, in the way I have described, is the technique for being able to be completely awake, to be like a buddha in any realm that exists. If you start to think what it would be like in some of those realms, you just thank your lucky stars that you're not in them, but if you were, you could still be there with an open heart. The essence of the practice is willingness to share pleasure and delight and the joy of life on the out-breath and willingness to feel your pain and that of others fully on the in-breath. That's the essence of it, and if you were never to receive any other instruction, that would be enough.

Now for the instruction. The first step is called "flashing absolute bodhicitta," which basically means just opening up. The second step is working with the abstract quality of pain by visualizing it as black, heavy, and hot, and breathing that in, and working with the abstract quality of pleasure by visualizing it as white, light, and cool, and breathing that out. My understanding of this stage is that before you get into the real meaty, difficult stuff, you work with the abstract principles of pain and pleasure, synchronizing them with the in-breath and the out-breath. The first stage is just open space. Then you start working with what's called the relative practice—the humanness, our everyday life situation—breathing pain in, pleasure out, black in, white out. Then you get to the third stage, which is actually the heart of the practice. Here you visualize a specific life situation and connect with the pain of it. You breathe that in, feeling it completely. It's the opposite of avoidance. You are completely willing to acknowledge and feel pain—your own pain, the pain of a dear friend, or the pain of a total stranger—and on the out-breath, you let the sense of ventilating and opening, the sense of spaciousness, go out.

In other words, suppose there's someone in your life that you can't stand, the very thought of whom brings up all kinds of negative feelings. You decide to do tonglen to work with feeling more open and brave and gentle in that particular situation. So you think of that person and up come those awful feelings, and when you're breathing in, you connect with them— their quality and texture and just how they grab your heart. It's not that you try to figure them out; you just feel the pain. Then on the out-breath you relax, let go, open up, ventilate the whole thing. But you don't luxuriate in that for very long because when you breathe in again, it's back to the painful feeling. You don't get completely trapped, drowned in *that*, be- cause next you breathe out—you open and relax and share some sense of space again. Maybe you want to grasp on to the joy, but then you breathe in again. Maybe you want to dwell in the pain, but then you breathe out again. It's like you're learning how to touch and go—you touch again and then you let go again. You don't prefer the pain to the pleasure or the pleasure to the pain; you go back and forth continually.

After you've worked with the specific object for a while and you are genuinely connecting with the pain and your ability to open and let go, then you take the practice a step further—you do it for all sentient beings. This is a key point about tonglen: your own experience of pleasure and pain becomes the way that you recognize your kinship with all sentient beings, the way you can share in the joy and the sorrow of everyone who's ever lived, everyone who's living now, and everyone who will ever live. You are acknowledging that the discomfort that you feel when you think of that particular person is something that all human beings feel, and the joy that you feel, the sense of being able to open up and let go, is also people's birthright. You're breathing in that same pain, but now you think to yourself, "Let me feel it so that no one else on the whole earth has to feel it." In other words, it becomes useful. "I'm miserable, I'm depressed. Okay. Let me feel it fully so that nobody else has to feel it, so that others could be free of it." It starts to awaken your heart because you have this aspiration to say, "This pain can be of benefit to others because I can be courageous enough to feel it fully so no one else has to." On the out-breath you say, "Let me give away something good or true that I ever feel, any sense of humor, any sense of enjoying the sun coming up and going down, any sense of delight in the world at all, so that everybody else may share in this and feel it."

So again, the first step is flashing some sense of openness and spaciousness, the second step is working with black in and white out, the third step is contacting something very real for us, and the fourth step is extending it out and being willing to do it for all sentient beings.

An interesting thing happens whenever I give tonglen instruction: people start going to sleep. It's hard to hear this stuff. I've never given tonglen instruction where I don't notice that at least three people are completely gone, and the others are probably all feeling extremely drowsy. By the same token, when you actually start doing the practice, you'll probably fall asleep a lot. Don't consider that an obstacle. This practice will still introduce to you the whole idea that you can feel both suffering and joy—that both are part of being human. If people are willing even for one second a day to make an aspiration to use their own pain and pleasure to help others, they are actually able to do it that much more. As you become more fearless, your bodhicitta will ripen with each day of your life, which will be of great benefit to others.

13
Taking Refuge

TODAY I WANT to talk about taking refuge in the
three jewels—the buddha, the dharma, and the
sangha—and what that really means.

When we're helpless infants, we totally depend on
others to take care of us; oterwise we couldn't eat
and we wouldn't be clean. If it were not for our help-
lessness, there would be no nurturing. Ideally, that
period of nurturing is one in which maitri, loving-
kindness, can be fostered in us. The Shambhala
teachings tell us that the young warrior, the baby
warrior, is placed in a cradle of loving-kindness. Ideally, among people striving to create an enlightened
society, in the period of nurturing, individuals would
naturally develop loving-kindness and respect toward
themselves and a sense of feeling relaxed and at
home with themselves. That would be a ground. In
an enlightened society, there would be some ceremonial rite of passage, such as many traditional peoples
have had, in which the child formally becomes a
young man or a young woman. It seems that too often
we're victims of not enough nurturing in the beginning, and we don't know when we've grown up. Some
of us at the age of fifty or sixty or seventy are still

wondering what we're going to be when we grow up.
We remain children in our heart of hearts, which is
to say, fundamentally theists.

In any case, whether we feel that we weren't nurtured properly, or whether we feel fortunate that we
were—whatever our situation—in the present moment we can always realize that the ground is to develop loving-kindness toward ourselves. As adults,
we can begin to cultivate a sense of loving-kindness
for ourselves—by ourselves, for ourselves. The whole
process of meditation is one of creating that good
ground, that cradle of loving-kindness where we actually are nurtured. What's being nurtured is our
confidence in our own wisdom, our own health, and
our own courage, our own goodheartedness. We develop some sense that the way we are—the kind of
personality that we have and the way we express
life—is good, and that by being who we are completely and by totally accepting that and having respect for ourselves, we are standing on the ground of
warriorship.

I've always thought that the phrase "to take refuge"
is very curious because it sounds theistic, dualistic,
and dependent "to take refuge" in something. I remember very clearly, at a time of enormous stress in
my life, reading *Alice in Wonderland*. Alice became a
heroine for me because she fell into this hole and she
just free-fell. She didn't grab for the edges, she wasn't
terrified, trying to stop her fall; she just fell and she

looked at things as she went down. Then, when she landed, she was in a new place. She didn't take refuge in anything. I used to aspire to be like that because I saw myself getting near the hole and just screaming, holding back, not wanting to go anywhere where there was no hand to hold.

In every human life (whether there are puberty rites or not) you are born, and you are born alone. You go through that birth canal alone, and then you pop out alone, and then a whole process begins. And when you die, you die alone. No one goes with you. The journey that you make, no matter what your belief about that journey is, is made alone. The fundamental idea of taking refuge is that between birth and death we are alone. Therefore, taking refuge in the buddha, the dharma, and the sangha does not mean finding consolation in them, as a child might find consolation in Mommy and Daddy. Rather, it's a basic expression of our aspiration to leap out of the nest, whether you feel ready for it or not, to go through your puberty rites and be an adult with no hand to hold. It expresses your realization that the only way to begin the real journey of life is to feel the ground of loving-kindness and respect for yourself and then to leap. In some sense, however, we never get to the point where we feel one hundred percent sure: "I have had my nurturing cradle. It's finished. Now I can leap." We are always continuing to develop maitri and continuing to leap. The other day I was talking about meeting our edge and our desire to grab on to something when we reach our limits. Then we see that there's more loving-kindness, more respect for ourselves, more confidence that needs to be nurtured. We work on that and we just keep leaping.

So for us, taking refuge means that we feel that the way to live is to cut the ties, to cut the umbilical cord and alone start the journey of being fully human, without confirmation from others. Taking refuge is the way that we begin cultivating the openness and the goodheartedness that allow us to be less and less dependent. We might say, "We shouldn't be dependent anymore, we should be open," but that isn't the point. The point is that you begin where you are, you see what a child you are, and you don't criticize that. You begin to explore, with a lot of humor and generosity toward yourself, all the places where you cling, and every time you cling, you realize, "Ah! This is where, through my mindfulness and my tonglen and everything that I do, my whole life is a process of learning how to make friends with myself." On the other hand, this need to cling, this need to hold the hand, this cry for Mom, also shows you that *that's* the edge of the nest. Stepping through right there—making a leap—becomes the motivation for cultivating maitri. You realize that if you can step through that doorway, you're going forward, you're becoming more of an adult, more of a complete person, more whole.

In other words, the only real obstacle is ignorance.

When you say "Mom!" or when you need a hand to hold, if you refuse to look at the whole situation, you aren't able to see it as a teaching—an inspiration to realize that this is the place where you could go further, where you could love yourself more. If you *can't* say to yourself at that point, "I'm going to look into this, because that's all I need to do to continue this journey of going forward and opening more," then you're committed to the obstacle of ignorance.

Working with obstacles is life's journey. The warrior is always coming up against dragons. Of course the warrior gets scared, particularly before the battle. It's frightening. But with a shaky, tender heart the warrior realizes that he or she is just about to step into the unknown, and then goes forth to meet the dragon. The warrior realizes that the dragon is nothing but unfinished business presenting itself, and that it's fear that really needs to be worked with. The dragon is just a motion picture that appears there, and it appears in many forms: as the lover who jilted us, as the parent who never loved us enough, as someone who abused us. Basically what we work with is our fear and our holding back, which are not necessarily obstacles. The only obstacle is ignorance, this refusal to look at our unfinished business. If every time the warrior goes and meets the dragon, he or she says, "Hah! It's a dragon again. No way am I going to face this," and just splits, then life becomes a recurring story of getting up in the morning, going out, meeting the dragon, saying, "No way," and splitting. In that case you become more and more timid and more and more afraid and more of a baby. No one's nurturing you, but you're still in that cradle, and you never go through your puberty rites.

So we say we take refuge in the buddha, we take refuge in the dharma, we take refuge in the sangha. In the oryoki meal chant we say, "The buddha's virtues are inconceivable, the dharma's virtues are inconceivable, the sangha's virtues are inconceivable," and "I prostrate to the buddha, I prostrate to the dharma, I prostrate to the sangha, I prostrate respectfully and always to these three." Well, we aren't talking about finding comfort in the buddha, dharma, and sangha. We aren't talking about prostrating in order to be safe. The buddha, we say traditionally, is the example of what we also can be. The buddha is the awakened one, and we too are the buddha. It's simple. We are the buddha. It's not just a way of speaking. We are the awakened one, meaning one who continually leaps, one who continually opens, one who continually goes forward. It isn't easy and it's accompanied by a lot of fear, a lot of resentment, and a lot of doubt. That's what it means to be human, that's what it means to be a warrior. To begin with, when you leave the cradle of loving-kindness, you are in this beautiful suit of armor because, in some sense, you're well protected and you feel safe. Then you go through puberty rites, the process of taking off the armor that you might have had some illusion was protecting you from something, only to find that actually it's shielding you from being fully alive and fully awake. Then you go forward and you meet the dragon, and every meeting shows you where there's still some armor to take off.

Taking refuge in the buddha means that you are willing to spend your life acknowledging or reconnecting with your awakeness, learning that every time you meet the dragon you take off more armor, particularly the armor that covers your heart. That's what we're doing here during this dathun, removing armor, removing our protections, undoing all the stuff that covers over our wisdom and our gentleness and our awake quality. We're not trying to be something we aren't; rather, we're rediscovering, reconnecting with who we are. So when we say, "I take refuge in the buddha," that means I take refuge in the courage and the potential of fearlessness of removing all the armor that covers this awakeness of mine. I am awake; I will spend my life taking this armor off. Nobody else can take it off because nobody else knows where all the little locks are, nobody else knows where it's sewed it up tight, where it's going to take a lot of work to get that particular iron thread untied. I may have a zipper that goes right down the front and has padlocks all the way down. Every time I meet the dragon, I take off as many padlocks as I can; eventually, I'll be able to take the zipper down. I might say to you, "Simple.

When you meet the dragon you just take off one of your padlocks and then your zipper'll come down." And you say, "What is she talking about?" because *you* have sewn a seam up under your left arm with iron thread. Every time *you* meet the dragon, you have to get out these special snippers that you have hidden away in a box with all your precious things and snip a few of those threads off, as many as you dare, until you start vomiting with fear and say, "This is enough for now." Then you begin to be much more awake and more connected with your buddha nature, with buddha—you know what it means to take refuge in buddha. To the next person you meet, you say, "It's easy. All you have to do is get your little snippers out of your precious box and you start—" and they look at you and they say, "What is he talking about?" because *they* have these big boots that come all the way up and cover their whole body and head. The only way to get the boots off is to start with the soles of the boots, and they know that every time they meet the dragon, they actually have to start peeling. So you have to do it alone. The basic instruction is simple: Start taking off that armor. That's all anyone can tell you. No one can tell you how to do it because you're the only one who knows how you locked yourself in there to begin with.

Taking refuge in the dharma is, traditionally, taking refuge in the teachings of the Buddha. Well, the teachings of the Buddha are: Let go and open to your world. Realize that trying to protect your territory, trying to keep your territory enclosed and safe, is fraught with misery and suffering. It keeps you in a very small, dank, smelly, introverted world that gets more and more claustrophobic and more and more misery-producing as you get older. As you get older, it is harder and harder to find the doorways out. When I was about twelve I read a *Life* magazine series, "Religions of the World." The article on Confucius said something like: "By the time you're fifty, if you've spent your life up until then taking the armor off [Confucius expressed this in his own language], then you've established a pattern of mind that for the rest of your life, you won't be able to stop. You'll just keep taking the armor off. But if by the time you're fifty you've become really good at keeping that armor on, keeping your zipper zipped up at any cost, keeping those boots on at any cost, then no matter what, you might be in the middle of an earthquake shattering into pieces, and if somehow you get it back together, then after that it's going to be very hard to change." Whether that's true or not, it scared me to death when I was twelve years old. It became a prime motivation for my life. I was determined somehow to grow rather than to become stuck.

So taking refuge in the dharma—teachings of the Buddha—is what it's all about. From a broader perspective, the dharma also means your whole life. The teachings of the Buddha are about letting go and opening: you do that in how you relate to the people in your life, how you relate to the situations you're in, how you relate with your thoughts, how you relate with your emotions. The purpose of your whole life is not to make a lot of money, it's not to find the perfect marriage, it's not to build Gampo Abbey. It's not to do any of these things. You have a certain life, and whatever life you're in is a vehicle for waking up. If you're a mother raising your children, that's the vehicle for waking up. If you're an actress, that's the vehicle for waking up. If you're a construction worker, that's the vehicle for waking up. If you're a retired person facing old age, that's the vehicle for waking up. If you're alone and you feel lonely and you wish you had a mate, that's the vehicle for waking up. If you have a huge family around you and wish you had a little more free time, that's the vehicle for waking up. Whatever you have, that's it. There's no better situation than the one you have. It's made for you. It'll show you everything you need to know about where your zipper's stuck and where you can leap. So that's what it means to take refuge in the dharma. It has to do with finding open space, not being covered in armor.

Taking refuge in the sangha is very much the same thing. It does not mean that we join a club where we're all good friends, talk about Buddhism together, nod sagely, and criticize the people who don't believe the way we do. Taking refuge in the sangha means taking refuge in the brotherhood and sisterhood of people who are committed to taking off their armor. If we live in a family where all the members are committed to taking off their armor, then one of the most powerful vehicles of learning how to do it is the feedback that we give one another, the kindness that we show to one another. Normally when somebody is feeling sorry for herself and beginning to wallow in it, people pat her on the back and say, "Oh, you poor thing," or "For Pete's sake, get off it." But if you yourself are committed to taking off your armor and you know that the other person is too, there is a way that you can actually give them the gift of dharma. With great kindness and love, out of your own experience of what's possible, you give them the wisdom that somebody else probably gave you the day before when *you* were miserable. You encourage them not to buy into their self-pity but to realize that it's an opportunity to grow, and that everybody goes through this experience. In other words, the sangha are people committed to helping one another to take off their armor, by not encouraging their weakness or their tendency to keep their armor on. When we see each other collapsing or stubbornly saying, "No, I like this armor," there's an opportunity to say something about the fact that underneath all that armor are a lot of festering sores, and a little bit of sunlight wouldn't hurt a bit. That's the notion of taking refuge in the sangha.

Taking refuge in the three jewels is no refuge at all from the conventional point of view. It's like finding a desert island in the middle of the ocean after a shipwreck—"Whew! Land!"—and "then standing there and watching it being eaten away, day by day, by the ocean. That's what taking refuge in the buddha, the dharma, and the sangha is like.

When we realize the need to take off our armor, we can take refuge in our awakeness and our aspiration not to cover it over any longer by taking refuge in the buddha. We can take refuge in the teachings of the Buddha and we can take refuge in the sangha, our family, those people committed to following the Buddha's teachings, with whom we can share support and inspiration.

Trungpa Rinpoche gave a definition of taking refuge that was pinned up on our bulletin board the other day. It begins with an absolute statement: "Since all things are naked, clear from obscurations, there is nothing to attain or realize." But then Rinpoche goes further and makes it very practical. "The everyday practice is simply to develop a complete acceptance and openness to all situations and emotions and all people. A complete acceptance and openness to all situations and emotions and to all people, experiencing everything totally without reservations or blockages, so that one never withdraws or centralizes into oneself." That is why we practice.

14

Not Preferring Samsara
or Nirvana

THIS MORNING I'd like to talk about not preferring samsara or nirvana.* Many of the *maha-
mudra*† teachings on the nature of mind talk about
stillness and occurrence. If you wanted to pare phe-
nomena down, all there would be are stillness and
occurrence: space, and that which is continually
born out of space, and returns into space—stillness
and occurrence. Sometimes it's called the back-
ground and the foreground. In any case, what I'd like
to talk about is not preferring stillness or occurrence,
or, you could say, not preferring the busyness of samsara or the stillness of nirvana.

Usually there is some kind of bias. There are two
common forms of human neurosis. One is getting all
caught up in worry and fear and hope, in wanting and
not wanting, and things: jobs, families, romances,

---

*Samsara is the vicious cycle of existence; nirvana is the cessation of
ignorance and of conflicting emotions, and therefore freedom from
compulsive rebirth in samsara.

†The state in which all experiences are transformed into transcenden-
tal knowledge and skillful means.

houses, cars, money, vacations, entertainment, the mountains, the desert, Europe, Mexico, Jamaica, the Black Hole of Calcutta, prison, war or peace, and so on. So many of us are caught in all that occurs, somehow captured by occurrence as if we were caught in a whirlpool. In samsara we continually try to get away from the pain by seeking pleasure, and in doing so, we just keep going around and around and around. I'm so hot I open all the windows, and then I'm so cold I put on a sweater. Then it itches, so I put cream on my arms, and then that's sticky, so I go take a bath. Then I'm cold, so I close the window, and on and on and on. I'm lonely, so I get married, and then I'm always fighting with my husband or my wife, so I start another love affair, and then my wife or husband threatens to leave me and I'm caught in the confusion of what to do next, and on and on and on. We are always trying to get out of the boiling pot into some kind of coolness, always trying to escape and therefore never really fully settling down and appreciating. That's called samsara. In other words, somehow we have this preference for occurrence, so we're always working in that framework of trying to get comfortable through political beliefs and philosophies and religions and everything, trying to gain pleasure in all that occurs.

The other neurosis—which is just as common—is to get caught by peace and quiet, or liberation, or freedom. When I was traveling, I met some people who had formed a group based on their belief that a flying saucer was going to come and take them away from all of this. They were waiting for the flying saucers to come and liberate them from the grossness of this earth. They talked about transcending the awfulness of life, getting into the space and the clarity and the blissfulness of not being hindered in any way, just completely free. When the spaceship took them away, they were going to a place where there weren't going to be any problems. This is what we all do in a subtle way. If we have an experience of clarity or bliss, we want to keep it going. That's what a lot of addiction is about, wanting to feel good forever, but it usually ends up not working out. However, it's a very common neurosis, being caught by this wanting to stay out there, wanting to stay in the space, like some friends of mine in the seventies who decided to take LSD every day so they could just stay out there. Sometimes that's expressed by arranging your life in such a way that it's very quiet, very smooth, very simplified; you become so attached to it that you just want to keep it like that. You resist and resent any kind of noisy situation like a lot of children or dogs coming in and messing everything up. There are some people who have tremendous insight into the nature of reality as vast and wonderful—what is sometimes called sacred outlook—but then they become completely dissatisfied with ordinary life. Rather than that glimpse of sacred outlook actually enriching their life, it makes them feel more poverty-stricken all the time. Often the reason that people go from necrosis into psychosis is that they see that spaciousness and synchronistic situation and how vast things are and how the world actually works, but then they cling to their insight and they become completely caught there. It has been said, quite accurately, that a psychotic person is drowning in the very same things that a mystic swims in.

What I'm saying here is that ego can use anything to re-create itself, whether it's occurrence or spaciousness, whether it's what we call samsara or what we call nirvana. There is a bias in many religious groups toward wanting to get away from the earth and the pain of the earth and never having to experience this awfulness again—"Let's just leave it behind and rest in nirvana." You may have noticed in our oryoki meal chant that we say the Buddha "does not abide in nirvana. He abides in the ultimate perfection." One could assume that if he does not abide in nirvana, the ultimate perfection must be some sense of completely realizing that samsara and nirvana are one, not preferring stillness or occurrence but being able to live fully with both.

Recently, in a friend's kitchen I saw on the wall a quotation from one of Chögyam Trungpa Rinpoche's talks, which said: "Hold the sadness and pain of samsara in your heart and at the same time the power and vision of the Great Eastern Sun. Then the warrior can make a proper cup of tea." I was struck by it because when I read it I realized that I myself have some kind of preference for stillness. The notion of holding the sadness and pain of samsara in my heart rang true, but I realized I didn't do that; at least, I had a definite preference for the power and vision of the Great Eastern Sun. My reference point was always to be awake and to live fully, to remember the Great Eastern Sun—the quality of being continually awake. But what about holding the sadness and pain of samsara in my heart at the same time? The quotation really made an impression on me. It was completely true: if you can live with the sadness of human life (what Rinpoche often called the tender heart or genuine heart of sadness), if you can be willing to feel fully and acknowledge continually your own sadness and the sadness of life, but at the same time not be drowned in it, because you also remember the vision and power of the Great Eastern Sun, you experience balance and completeness, joining heaven and earth, joining vision and practicality. We talk about men and women joining heaven and earth, but really they are already joined. There isn't any separation between samsara and nirvana, between the sadness and pain of samsara and the vision and power of the Great Eastern Sun. One can hold them both in one's heart, which is actually the purpose of practice. As a result of that, one can make a proper cup of tea.

Ritual is about joining vision and practicality, heaven and earth, samsara and nirvana. When things are properly understood, one's whole life is like a ritual or a ceremony. Then all the gestures of life are *mudra** and all the sounds of life are *mantra*†— sacredness is everywhere. This is what's behind ritual, these formallized things that get carried down in the religions of different cultures. Ritual, when it's heartfelt, is like a time capsule. It's as if thousands of years ago somebody had a clear, unobstructed view of magic, power, and sacredness, and realized that if he went out each morning and greeted the sun in a very stylized way, perhaps by doing a special chant and making offerings and perhaps by bowing, that it connected him to that richness. Therefore he taught his children to do that, and the children taught their children, and so on. So thousands of years later, people are still doing it and connecting with exactly the same feeling. All the rituals that get handed down are like that. Someone can have an insight, and rather than its being lost, it can stay alive through ritual. For example, Rinpoche often said that the dharma, the teachings of the Buddha, are like a recipe for fresh-baked bread. Thousands of years ago someone discovered how to bake bread, and because the recipe was passed down for years and years, you can still make fresh bread that you can eat right now.

---

*Symbolic hand gestures that accompany tantric practices to state the quality of different moments of meditation.

†Words or syllables that express the quintessence of various energies.

What made me think of ritual as the joining of the sadness and pain of samsara with the vision of the Great Eastern Sun was that somehow it's simply using ordinary things to express our appreciation for life. The sun comes up in the morning, we can use the sound of a gong to call us to the shrine room, we can put our hands together in *gassho* and bow to each other, we can hold up our oryoki bowls with three fingers in the same way that people have been doing for centuries. Through these rituals we express our appreciation for the fact that there's food and objects and the richness of the world. You hold your bowl up, and then at the end of dathun you go home and perhaps you forget all about oryoki. Maybe you come back years later and do another program, and you find there's something touching about doing it again. Perhaps you did it first when you were twenty years old, and then suddenly at eighty you find yourself doing it again. It's like a thread running through your whole life, holding up your oryoki bowl with three fingers.

Genuine, heartfelt ritual helps us reconnect with power and vision as well as with the sadness and pain of the human condition. When the power and vision come together, there's some sense of doing things properly for their own sake. Making a proper cup of tea means that you thoroughly and completely make that tea because you appreciate the tea and the boiling water and the fact that together they make something that's nourishing and delicious, that lifts one's spirit. You don't do it because you're worried that someone's not going to like you if you don't do it right. Nor do you do it so fast that it's over before you even realize that you made a cup of tea, let alone that you drank six cups. So whether it's smoking a cigarette or drinking a cup of tea or making your bed or washing the dishes—whatever it might be—it's ritual in the sense of doing it properly, if you can hold the sadness in your heart as well as the vision of the Great Eastern Sun.

Chögyam Trungpa, Rinpoche, loved ritual. He drew from all traditions—including Tibetan, Japanese, and British—to create rituals, one of which was how he would walk into the shrine room. You would be sitting in the shrine room and then suddenly you would hear the crack of the ceremonial sticks (*gandi*), the ping of the small gong, and the boom of the big drum: "crack," "ping," "boom," "crack," "ping," "boom." As the sound gradually came closer and closer, you knew that Rinpoche was just about to enter. Then there he was, with his procession of attendants. He was just entering the shrine room to give his talks, but somehow the ritual of it created an environment in which the space would open up. You felt as if you were in a timeless space. It wasn't June 22, 1989; it was no particular time of day or night or calendar year, it was just space. He knew that if he created all these sounds and rituals, all of us would benefit from that experience of timelessness.

Native peoples have always understood about the

seasons, the sun coming up and going down, and the earth, and they have rituals to celebrate all those things. So that no one can miss the fact that we are all connected, puberty rites and all the other ceremonies are well choreographed, like a beautiful dance. The old people know how to do these things and they pass the knowledge on, and that's called lineage. Black Elk was a Sioux holy man in the 1880s, a time when his people were losing heart, losing their spirit, because the way they had always lived, which had given them so much sense of being connected, was being destroyed. Yet it was still early enough that they had not lost all of it. When he was nine years old, he had a vision of how he might save his people, a vision about horses coming from the four directions. In one direction the horses were white, in another direction sorrel, in another direction buckskin, in the last direction black. With them came maidens carring sacred objects, and the grandfathers singing prophecies. Each direction had its whole ritualistic symbolism. He never told his vision to anyone, because he thought nobody would believe him. But when he was about seventeen years old, he felt he was going a little crazy, so he finally told the medicine man, who immediately understood and said, "We have to act it out." They did the whole thing, painting their bodies in the way he had seen, enacting the entire vision.

When he was in his twenties, things had completely fallen apart. He ended up being in Buffalo

Bill's Wild West Show, with some other Indians. They were taken on a "fire-boat" to Europe to do a show in London with all their ponies and their Indian clothing. One night Queen Victoria came to see the show. Now, you wouldn't think there would be much in common between Black Elk, an Oglala Sioux from the Plains in 1886, and Queen Victoria, but that night nobody else came—just Queen Victoria in a shining carriage and her entourage. When the show was finished, she stood up and shook hands with all of them with her little soft hand. He really liked her. Then she bowed to them, and they were so impressed with her and her bearing that the women did something called the tremolo and the men did the whooping, and then they all bowed to her. Black Elk described her as "Grandmother England." She had so much majesty and presence. "She was little and fat and she was good to us." About a month later, she invited them to her Silver Jubilee. As he said, when he and the other native people got to this great big building, everyone was yelling, "Jubilee! Jubilee! Jubilee!" He said he still didn't know what that meant, but then he was able to describe what he saw. First in her golden coach came Queen Victoria, the horses all covered in gold and her clothes all gold like fire. Then in the black coach with the black horses was the queen's grandson, and in the black coach with the gray horses were her relatives. He described all the coaches and all the horses and then all the men arriving in their beautiful clothing, riding on black horses with plumes. The whole ceremony meant something to them. He said that before the Jubilee he felt like a man who had never had a vision, but that seeing all that pomp and circumstance reconnected him with his heart. When Queen Victoria in her golden coach came by the Indians, she had the coach stopped and she stood up and she bowed to them again. Again they threw all their things in the air and whooped and hollered and did the tremolo, and then they sang to Grandmother England. It cheered them up.

Ritual can be the Queen of England or the people of the Great Plains. It somehow transcends time and space. In any case, I think it has something to do with holding the sadness and pain of samsara in your heart and at the same time holding the vision and power of the Great Eastern Sun. Our whole life could be a ritual. We could learn to stop when the sun goes down and when the sun comes up. We could learn to listen to the wind; we could learn to notice that it's raining or snowing or hailing or calm. We could reconnect with the weather that is ourselves, and we could realize that it's sad. The sadder it is, the vaster it is, and the vaster it is, the more our heart opens. We can stop thinking that good practice is when it's smooth and calm, and bad practice is when it's rough and dark. If we can hold it all in our hearts, then we can make a proper cup of tea.

15

The Dharma That Is Taught and the Dharma That Is Experienced

TRADITIONALLY, there are two ways of describing the teachings of the Buddha: the dharma that is taught and the dharma that is experienced. The dharma that is taught has been presented continuously in books and lectures in a pure and fresh way since the time of the Buddha. Even though it all began in India, in a very different kind of time and space and culture than we know today, the essence of the teachings was capable of transmission to Southeast Asia, Japan, China, Korea, Vietnam, and Tibet—to all the places to which Buddhism has spread—by people who could express what they themselves had been taught. Nowadays there are so many wonderful books on the basic teachings; you can read Joseph Goldstein and Ayya Khema and Suzuki Roshi and Chögyam Trungpa and Tarthang Tülku and all the translations of Herbert Guenther. There are so many different ways you can read and hear the teachings, and they all have slightly different flavors. But you will find that if in each one you choose a theme, like the four noble truths or loneliness or compassion, they all say the same thing about it, according to their own style or culture. The teachings are the same and the essence is the same.

The dharma that is taught is like a jewel, a precious jewel. Like bodhicitta, it can be covered over by dirt and yet is unchanged by dirt. When someone brings the jewel out into the light and shows it to everyone, it resonates in the hearts and minds of those who see it. The teachings are also like a beautiful golden bell hidden away in a deep, dark cave; when someone brings it out and rings it, people can hear the sound. That's the dharma that is taught. Traditionally it is said that the dharma can be taught, but one has to have ears to hear it. The analogy of three pots is given. If you're like a pot with a big hole in the bottom, then when the dharma is put in, it just goes right out. If you're like a pot that has poison in it, when the dharma is put in, it gets reinterpreted and comes out as poison. In other words, if you're full of resentment and bitterness, you might reinterpret it to suit your own bitterness and resentment. If the pot is turned upside down, nothing can be put into the pot. You have to be awake and open to hear the dharma that is taught.

The dharma that is experienced is not a different dharma, although sometimes it feels quite different. A common experience is that when you hear the teachings, they resonate in your heart and mind, and you feel inspired by them, but you can't figure out what they have to do with your everyday life. When push comes to shove and you lose your job or the person you love leaves you or something else happens and your emotions go crazy and wild, you can't quite figure out what that has to do with the four noble truths. Your pain feels so intense that the four noble truths seem somewhat pitiful by comparison. Trungpa Rinpoche once said that the dharma has to be experienced because when the real quality of our lives, including the obstacles and problems and experiences that cause us to start questioning, becomes intense, any mere philosophical belief isn't going to hold a candle to the reality of what we are experiencing.

What you will discover as you continue to study the dharma and to practice meditation is that nothing that you have ever heard is separate from your life. Dharma is the study of what *is*, and the only way you can find out what is true is through studying yourself. The Zen master Dogen said, "To know yourself or study yourself is to forget yourself, and if you forget yourself then you become enlightened by all things." Knowing yourself or studying yourself just means that it's *your* experience of joy, it's *your* experience of pain, *your* experience of relief and ventilation, and *your* experience of sorrow. That's all we have and that's all we need in order to have a living experience of the dharma—to realize that the dharma and our lives are the same thing.

I'm so struck by the quotation that appeared on the bulletin board yesterday. It said, "The everyday practice is simply to develop complete acceptance and openness to all situations, emotions, and people." You read that and you hear it and maybe I even talk about it, but basically, what does that mean? When you read it, you think you sort of know what it means, but when you begin to try to do that, to test it against your experience, then your preconceptions of what it means completely fall apart; you discover something fresh and new that you never realized before. What personal identification with the dharma means is, live that way, test it, try to find out what it really means in terms of losing your job, being jilted by your lover, dying of cancer. "Be open and accept all situations and people." How do you do that? Maybe that's the worst advice anybody could give you, but you have to find out for yourself.

Often we hear the teachings so subjectively that we think we're being told what is true and what is false. But the dharma never tells you what is true or what is false. It just encourages you to find out for yourself. However, because we have to use words, we make statements. For example, we say, "The everyday practice is simply to develop complete acceptance of all situations, emotions, and people." That sounds like that's what's true and not to do that would be false. But that's not what it says. What it does say is to encourage you to find out for yourself what is true and what is false. Try to live that way and see what happens. You'll come up against all your doubts and fears and your hopes and you'll grapple with that. When you start to live that way, with that sense of "What does this really mean?," you'll find it quite interesting. After a while, you forget that you're even asking the question; you just practice meditation or you just live your life, and you have what is traditionally called insight, which means that you have a fresh take on what is true. Insight comes suddenly, as though you've been wandering around in the dark and someone switches on all the lights and reveals a palace. You say, "Wow! it's always been here." Yet insight is very simple; it isn't always "Wow!" It's as if all your life there's been this bowl of white stuff sitting on your table but you don't know what it is. You're sort of scared to find out. Maybe it's LSD, or cocaine, or rat poison. One day you moisten your finger, you touch it and get a few little grains, and you taste it, and my goodness, it's salt. Nobody can tell you otherwise—it's so obvious, so simple, so clear. So we all have insights. In our meditation we have them and perhaps we share them. I suppose that's what all these talks are, sharing insights. It feels as if we've discovered something that no one else ever knew, and yet it's completely straightforward and simple.

You can never deny the dharma that is experienced because it's so straightforward and true. But traveling the path between the dharma that is taught and the

dharma that is experienced involves allowing yourself and encouraging yourself not to always believe
what you're taught, but to wonder about it. All you
have to do is to live that way and it will become your
path. The quotation on the bulletin board goes on to
say that the way to do this is to stay open and never
to withdraw. Never centralize into yourself. These
are not just sweet little aphorisms, but actually the
most profound teachings put in a deceptively simple
way. You might think, "Oh, yes, never withdraw, fine,
but what does that mean?" Obviously, it doesn't mean
that you're a bad person to withdraw; you've been
taught about maitri and loving-kindness and nonjudgmental attitude and acceptance of yourself, not
being afraid to be who you are. Do you see what I
mean? In *Zen Mind, Beginner's Mind* Suzuki Roshi
says that he got a letter from one of his students that
said, "Dear Roshi, you sent me a calendar and each
month has a very inspiring statement, but I'm not
even into February yet and I find that I can't measure
up to these statements." Suzuki Roshi was laughing
at the fact that people use the dharma to make themselves feel miserable. Or other people who have a
quick conceptual grasp of the dharma may use it to
become arrogant and proud. If you find yourself misunderstanding the teachings, the teachings themselves will always show you where you're off. In some
sense, the dharma is like a seamless web that you
can't get out of.

The dharma should really be taken to heart, not just used as a way to get cozy and secure or to continue your habitual pattern of self-denigration or your habitual pattern of striving for perfection. Initially you may find that you use the dharma as you've always used everything else, but then, because it's the dharma, it might occur to you that you're using it to denigrate yourself or to become a perfectionist—"Oh, my goodness! I'm using this to make the world into love and light or to make it a resentful, harsh place."

Trungpa Rinpoche told us that like most *tülkus*,* he was brought up extremely strictly. He was hit when he did things that weren't considered proper for a tülku to do, and he had to study very hard. He said he was a difficult boy and so he was punished a lot, but he was also smart and was quite proud of himself. His tutors never praised him; they always scolded him and told him he should work harder. Nevertheless, he could tell they were quite impressed with his brilliance. When it came time for him to start visiting his guru, Jamgon Kongtrul of Sechen, to review his studies, he couldn't wait to display his knowledge and intelligence. It was early morning and the light was shining through the window onto Jamgon Kongtrul's face. Rinpoche sat down next to him. Jamgon Kongtrul was very quiet for a while, and

---

*A tülku is the incarnation of a previous enlightened teacher, manifesting the spiritual qualities of that teacher.

finally he said, "Well, tell me what you know about all the six *paramitas*,*" and Rinpoche confidently rattled it all off with all the references and all the different things that different teachers had said. When it was all finished, Jamgon Kongtrul was quiet again, and then he said, "But what do you *feel* about all that?" Startled, Rinpoche said, "What does it matter what I feel about it? This is the way it's always been taught and it's been taught this way since it was first presented and this is how it is." Jamgon Kongtrul said, "It's all very well to know it intellectually, but how do you feel about it? What is your experience of this?" Rinpoche said that was how Jamgon Kongtrul always taught him. He always wanted to know what his experience of generosity or of discipline was, and so on. That was what Jamgon Kongtrul nurtured and cultivated in him.

In terms of the dharma that is taught, Trungpa Rinpoche heard it very well and very clearly. His own life had a tremendous amount of learning in it, and he always wanted us to learn and study as well. but he cared most that one should find the true meaning and not just accept another person's view without questioning it. When Rinpoche talked about the precepts, for example, he said it's all very well, you could know all two hundred and fifty or three hundred precepts

---

*The six paramitas, or "perfections," are generosity, discipline, patience, exertion, meditation, and knowledge.

by heart and all the references, but the crucial point was to get the true meaning of the precepts. For instance, you might know that the first precept is not to kill, and you may know all the stories of how that precept came into being, and you may know the logic of how killing increases ego-fixation and how working with the precepts cuts the chain of cause and effect— you may know all that, but the question really is, when the desire to kill something arises, why is it that you want to kill something? What's really going on there? And what would the benefit be of refraining from killing? What does refraining do? How do you feel when you refrain? What does it teach you? That's the way Rinpoche was trained, and that's the way he trained us.

The dharma that is taught and the dharma that is experienced are descriptions of how to live, how to use your life to wake you up rather than put you to sleep. And if you choose to spend the rest of your life trying to find out what awake means and what asleep means, I think you might attain enlightenment.

16

Sticking to One Boat

IN TRAVELING around and meeting so many people of so many different traditions as well as nontraditions, what I have found is that, in order to go deeper, there has to be some kind of whole-hearted commitment to truth or wanting to find out, wanting to find out what the *ngedön*, or true meaning, is. Therefore, if you want to hear the dharma, you can hear it from many different places, but you are uncommitted until you actually encounter a particular way that rings true in your heart and you decide to follow it. Then you make a connection with that particular lineage of teachings and that particular body of wisdom. Each religion or philosophical belief or New Age group has a kind of wisdom that it carries and explores. The point is that it's best to stick to one boat, so to speak, whatever that boat may be, because otherwise the minute you really begin to hurt, you'll just leave or you'll look for something else.

Recently I was asked to give a weekend program in a kind of New Age spiritual shopping mart. It was like a mall, with about seventy different things being presented. I got the first hit when I came to give my first talk. There was this great big poster, like a school bulletin board, that said, Basic Goodness, Room 606; Rolfing, Room 609; Astral Travel, Room 666; and so forth. I was one of many different things being of- fered. The people that you would meet in the parking lot or at lunch would say, "Oh, what are you taking this weekend?" It was very interesting because I hadn't encountered anything like that for a long time. Once I had been doing that myself; in order to stop, I had to hear Rinpoche say that shopping is actually always trying to find security, always trying to feel good about yourself. When one sticks to one boat, whatever that boat may be, then one actually begins the warrior's journey. So that's what I would recom- mend. I particularly want to say that because as you may have noticed, I myself am at this point some- what eclectic in my references and the things that inspire me, which might give you the impression that you could go to a Sun Dance one weekend and then to a weekend with Thich Nhat Hanh and then maybe to a Krishnamurti workshop. Basically it doesn't seem to work like that. It's best to stick with one thing and let it put you through your changes. When you have really connected with the essence of that and you already are on the journey, everything speaks to you and everything educates you. You don't feel chauvin- istic any longer, but you also know that your vehicle was the one that worked for you.

The way that Trungpa Rinpoche trained his stu- dents was a combination of the Kagyü and the Nyingma lineages of teachings of Tibetan Buddhism. When he first came to North America and began to teach, he really liked what he found here. He found that the students didn't know anything. He compared them to a herd of wild ponies or a kennel full of playful Labrador puppies. They were wide open, energetic, naive young people, most of whom had "dropped out" and had long hair and beards, no shirts, and no shoes. He liked that because it was very fertile ground. In England, where he had first encountered Western students, the people who were attracted to Buddhism were Buddhist scholars who couldn't hear the dharma because they couldn't let go of their preconceived ideas of how it fit in with preconceived scholarly notions. That was their obstacle, which he, I'm sure, enjoyed working with. The obstacle in North America was spiritual materialism. He gave many talks in the early days geared to this question; the first few chapters of his book *Cutting Through Spiritual Materialism* address it very directly. I would say that for four or five years practically the only teaching Rinpoche gave, in many different forms, under many different titles, was, "Stop shopping around and settle down and go deeply into one body of truth." He taught that this continual dabbling around in spiritual things was just another form of materialism, trying to get comfortable, trying to get secure, whereas if you stuck to one boat and really started working with it, it would definitely put you through all your changes. You would meet all your dragons; you would be continually pushed out of the nest. It would be one big initiation rite, and tremendous wisdom would come from that, tremendous heartfelt, genuine spiritual growth and development. One's life would be well spent. He stressed that his students should stop just dabbling in spirituality to try to feel good or get high or be spiritual. He was very cynical and knocked all kinds of "trips," as he called them; you can imagine the trips in North America in 1970. Many of us, we don't have to imagine that. We remember well—we're laboratory specimens!

17

Inconvenience

TODAY I'D LIKE to talk about inconvenience. When you hear some teachings that ring true to you, and you feel some trust in practicing that way and some trust in it's being a worthwhile way to live, then you're in for a lot of inconvenience. From an everyday perspective, it seems good to do things that are kind of convenient; there is no problem with that. It's just that when you really start to take the warrior's journey—which is to say, when you start to want to live your life fully instead of opting for death, when you begin to feel this passion for life and for growth, when discovery and exploration and curiosity become your path—then basically, if you follow your heart, you're going to find that it's often extremely inconvenient.

When you take refuge and become a Buddhist, you become a refugee. That is to say, you leave home and you become homeless in the absolute sense. Of course, you can still be living in a very nice place, surrounded by family and loved ones, or at least by your cats and dogs or squirrels or horses or the wind. Nevertheless, in your heart of hearts, once you start this journey there's the sense of leaving home and becoming homeless. Another image for that is the *bardo*:* you've left the shore, but you haven't arrived anywhere yet. You don't know where you're going, and you've been out there at sea long enough that you only have a vague memory of where you came from. You've left home, you've become homeless, you long to go back, but there's no way to go back. That's called the bardo, in-between. In some sense, I think, right now that's where we all are with this dathun. Even though we're still here, people are thinking about leaving and there's some sense of bardo, not quite here, not quite there, just hanging out in this sort of uneasy space and having to sit with it hour after hour. Your mind keeps going back and forth, but basically the instruction is just to leave home, label it "thinking," leave home and remain homeless with that sort of in-between feeling of, "It was so cozy here for a while. It will be cozy again when I get back, I think. Won't it? Will it?"

Since the day before yesterday, I myself have been feeling this bardo. We're still doing the dathun, and yet there's another program about to happen. I find myself getting jumpy and edgy and thinking I'm catching the flu and wondering why I'm dizzy and irritable. It's just bardo. We're still here, but where are we? It's so inconvenient. It's much more conve-

---

*An intermediate state. The term usually refers to the period between death and the next rebirth.

nient to be home. This particular boat that sails out
is no luxury liner. It's more like the boats that the
boat people from Vietnam were on—the pirates
might come at any moment, and you don't know if
you're ever going to reach the other shore or if the
food or the water is going to last. The situation doesn't
have to be grim, but it definitely has that feeling of,
"Is this where I was or where I'm going? Where is
this?" If you do shamatha practice properly—I don't
know what it means to do it properly, but let's say if
you do it for a while—sometimes you have that feeling of having left home totally and being homeless.
The breath goes out and where are you? Or sometimes there's this nice, cozy, or possibly uncomfortable but nevertheless solid reality in your mind, and
it's filling up all the space very successfully, and then
you wake up out of that dream and say, "Thinking,"
and you may wonder where are you and who are you
and what is it today? I can't remember, is it 1978 or—I
know it's not 2000 yet, but what year is it? With this
weather, what month is it, is it June? It feels a little
more like November—maybe it's August. What,
where, when? Refugee, you're called a refugee.

In *Born in Tibet*, Trungpa Rinpoche tells the story
of how he left Tibet at the time of the Chinese Com-
munist invasion. It's a vivid illustration of what being
a refugee is like. This great group of Tibetans, maybe
three hundred, including old people and babies and
everyone in between, left eastern Tibet—Kham—

with their guides. When they got to central Tibet, the guides didn't know the way any longer, because they knew only eastern Tibet. As a result, there weren't any guides to take them to India. Furthermore, the snow was so deep that it was up to their armpits, so the biggest monks went in front, prostrating their whole bodies in the snow and then getting up and prostrating again to make a path. At times they would go all the way up to the tops of mountains, only to find that they had made a mistake and would have to come all the way back down. They didn't have much food, and not only that, had they been discovered, they would have been shot by the Chinese. At one point they had to go through a river, and their clothes froze on them. Rinpoche said that if they tried to sit down, their *chubas* (dresses) and their robes cut their skin because the ice was so sharp. Not very convenient. Rinpoche said that as they walked along, they made a kind of clinking sound. He joked, "Oh, I hope the Chinese don't hear us, they might think it's some kind of code: clink, clink, clink." He said nobody else thought it was funny. (He tells stories again and again of making jokes about what was going on, and then he always says, "But nobody else thought it was funny.")

When this journey was finished, the refugees found themselves in India, homeless, in a completely alien climate. Many of them got tuberculosis right away from moving from a high, cold, clear place to a low, hot, dry, dusty place. Eventually Nehru's government was very kind to the Tibetans, but when they first came and even when the people were hospitable, the refugees were still homeless. Nobody knew who they were. There was no difference between a tülku or the head of a monastery and an ordinary person. Everyone's identity was somehow leveled.

Refugee: that's what it means to become a Buddhist, that's what it means to become one who wholeheartedly is using one's life to wake up instead of to go to sleep. It's very inconvenient. Trungpa Rinpoche was a man who appreciated the lessons of inconvenience; he was also a man who lived wholeheartedly. It didn't matter if it was convenient or inconvenient. There was some sense of wholehearted journey in his life. Once you know that the purpose of life is simply to walk forward and continually to use your life to wake you up rather than put you to sleep, then there's that sense of wholeheartedness about inconvenience, wholeheartedness about convenience.

Rinpoche emphasized inconvenience. For instance, he always kept everybody waiting for his talks, I don't think through any plan on his part, but simply because he was who he was. There was an *abhisheka* (empowerment ceremony) for which he kept people waiting for three days. It was often the case that when he would finally do something, you had so completely given up that you didn't think that it would ever really happen. When he wanted everyone to move to Nova Scotia, he used to tease people

about their comfort orientation. He said, "Oh, you're
not going to want to do it because it might mean leaving your nice house or your nice job. You might not
have an easy time finding a job in Nova Scotia."
Sometimes I think he wanted people to move to
Nova Scotia just because it was so inconvenient.
Comfort orientation murders the spirit—that was
the general message. Opting for coziness, having that
as your prime reason for existing, becomes a continual obstacle to taking a leap and doing something
new, doing something unusual, like going as a stranger
into a strange land.

Rinpoche's oldest son, the Sawang Ösel Mukpo,
told me that Rinpoche told him that he liked to ar-
range the furniture in his rooms so that it was just
slightly uncomfortable to reach for a glass. Instead of
putting the table close so that everything was comfortable, he liked it to be about half an inch too far
away so that you had to reach. Rinpoche also said
many times that it was good to wear your clothes a
little too tight. He himself used to wear an obi, the
wide belt that goes with a kimono, underneath his
clothes, really tight, so that if he slouched, he would
be uncomfortable—he had to keep his "head and
shoulders." He designed uniforms. I remember one
he designed to be worn at a certain ceremony: it was
made of scratchy wool with a high collar, and the
temperature outside was about ninety degrees with
high humidity as well. He contended that those in-

conveniences actually perk you up, keep you awake, present gaps in your cozy, seamless reality of centralizing into yourself.

When I was feeling a little off these last couple of days, it was like a prod to figure out, "What am I going to do, just cave in? Yeah, I'll just cave in. Who cares?" Then I noticed that other people began to feel uneasy because I had snapped at them. They hadn't done anything wrong; I was just feeling irritable. You realize that how you feel affects people, and yet you don't want to pretend that you feel good when actually you feel horrible. It's like a koan and you're left with it. If you're really wholehearted, you're continually left with this koan of inconvenience. It's so inconvenient to find that you're irritable, that you have a headache. It's inconvenient to get sick, so inconvenient to lose your great radiating presence and be just a normal shmuck. It's so inconvenient to have people not regard you as wonderful, so inconvenient to have people see that you have egg in your beard, that in the middle of the oryoki ceremony there's dental floss stuck to the bottom of your foot. It's so inconvenient to find yourself embarrassed, so inconvenient to find yourself not measuring up.

The very first teaching I ever got that I can remember was at a dharmadhatu, one of the centers Rinpoche established. One of the older students was giving a talk, and he began by saying, "If you are interested in these teachings, then you have to accept

the fact that you're never going to get it all together."
It was a shocking statement to me. He said with a lot
of clarity. "You are never going to get it all together,
you're never going to get your act togeth_r, fully, completely. You're never going to get all the little loose
ends tied up."

Life is so inconvenient. It's so inconvenient running this abbey, I can't tell you. You just get the
kitchen together and the bookkeeper leaves. You just
get the books together and the housekeeper leaves.
You just get a good housekeeper and a good kitchen
and a good bookkeeper, and suddenly there are no
monks or nuns in the monastery. Then maybe everything's working and the water goes off for a week and
there's no electricity and the food starts rotting. It's
so inconvenient.

Wholeheartedness is a precious gift, but no one
can actually give it to you. You have to find the path
that has heart and then walk it impeccably. In doing
that, you again and again encounter your own up-
tightness, your own headaches, your own falling flat
on your face. But in wholeheartedly practicing and
wholeheartedly following that path, this inconvenience is not an obstacle. It's simply a certain texture
of life, a certain energy of life. Not only that, sometimes when you just get flying and it all feels so good
and you think, "This is it, this is the path that has
heart," you suddenly fall flat on your face. Everybody's looking at you. You say to yourself, "What hap-

pened to that path that had heart? This feels like the path full of mud in my face." Since you are whole-heartedly committed to the warrior's journey, it pricks you, it pokes you. It's like someone laughing in your ear, challenging you to figure out what to do when you don't know what to do. It humbles you. It opens your heart.

18

The Four Reminders

THE TRADITIONAL four reminders are basic reminders of why one might make a continual effort to return to the present moment. The first one reminds us of our precious human birth; the second, of the truth of impermanence; the third, of the law of karma; and the fourth, of the futility of continuing to wander in samsara. Today I'd like to talk about these four ways of continually waking yourself up and remembering why you practice, why when you go home you might try to set up a space where you can meditate each day and just be fully with yourself the way you have been here for a month. Why even bother to wake up rather than go to sleep? Why spend the rest of your life sowing seeds of wakefulness, aspiring to take a leap and open up more and become a warrior? Why? When there are all these financial worries, marital problems, problems with friends, problems with communication, problems with everything, and you feel trapped, why bother to go and sit? Why bother to look up at the sky and try to find a gap or some space in that thick discursiveness? We ask ourselves these very basic questions all the time.

The teachings on the four reminders address these

questions. You can reflect on them any time, whether you live at Gampo Abbey or in Vancouver or in Minnesota, Chicago, New York City, the Black Hole of Calcutta, the top of Mount Everest, or the bottom of the ocean. Whether you're a *naga* (water-being) or a ghost or a human or a hell-being or a god-realm person—whatever you are—you can reflect on these four reminders of why you practice.

The first reminder is our precious birth. All of us sitting here have what is traditionally called a good birth, one that is rare and wonderful. All you have to do is pick up *Time* magazine and compare yourself to almost anyone on any page to realize that, even though you do have your miseries, your psychological unpleasantnesses, your feelings of being trapped, and so on, they're kind of rarefied compared with how it could be in terms of being run over by tanks, starving to death, being bombed, being in prison, being seriously addicted to alcohol or drugs or anything else that's self-destructive. The other day I read about a nineteen-year-old girl addicted to crack, nine months pregnant, whose life consists of shooting up and then going out to prostitute herself so she can get enough money to shoot up again. She was about to give birth to a baby who was going to be addicted to crack. That was her whole life; she would continue to do that until she died. On the other hand, living a cushy life in which everything is totally luxurious is also not at all helpful. You don't have the opportunity to develop much understanding about how people suffer or much sense of an open heart. You're all caught up in the good feeling of having two or three hundred pairs of shoes in your closet, like Imelda Marcos, or a beautiful home with a swimming pool, or whatever it is you have.

The basic thing is to realize that we have everything going for us. We don't have extreme pain that's inescapable. We don't have total pleasure that lulls us into ignorance. When we start feeling depressed, it's helpful to reflect on that. Maybe this is a good time to read the newspapers a lot and remember how terrifying life can be. We're always in a position where something might happen to us. We don't know. We're Jews living in France or Germany or Holland in 1936, we're just leading our ordinary lives, getting up in the morning, having our two or three meals a day, having our routines, and then one day the Gestapo comes and takes us away. Or maybe we're living in Pompeii and all of a sudden a volcano erupts and we're under a lot of lava. Anything could happen. Now is a very uncertain time. We don't know. Even at the personal level, tomorrow, any one of us might find that we have an incurable disease or that someone we love very much does.

In other words, life can just turn upside down. Anything can happen. How precious, how really sweet and precious our lives are. We are in the midst of this beauty, we have our health and intelligence and education and enough money and so forth, and yet every one of us has had our bout of depression during this dathun, every single one of us has had that feeling in the pit of our stomach. That definitely happens. One thing that Rinpoche taught and also really manifested to all of us who knew him—even though it's not easy to pull it off—was that just because you're feeling depressed doesn't mean that you have to forget how precious the whole situation is. Depression is just like weather—it comes and goes. Lots of different feelings, emotions, and thoughts, they just come and go forever, but that's no reason to forget how precious the situation is.

Beginnning to realize how precious life is becomes one of your most powerful tools. It's like gratitude. If you feel gratitude for your life, then even if the Nazi trucks come and take you away, you don't lose that feeling of gratitude. There's a mahayana slogan: "Be grateful to everyone." Basically, it doesn't matter how bad it gets, once you have this feeling of gratitude for your own life and the preciousness of human birth, then it takes you into any realm. What I'm saying is that *now* it's easy. If you think you can start feeling grateful when you're in the hell realm, if you think you can suddenly perk up, you'll find it's about five hundred percent more difficult than in our present situation; you'll have trouble doing it. We are actually in the best and the easiest situation. It's good to remember that. It's good to remember all the talks

you've ever heard on basic goodness and basic cheerfulness and gratitude.

In the vajrayana there's a lot of emphasis put on
devotion, which could be a form of immense gratitude that has a lot of vision in it. Devotion is remembering all those who worked so hard, who had the
same neurosis, the same pain that we do, the same
depression, the same toothaches, the same difficult
relationships, the same bills—the same everything—
who never gave up. Because they never gave up, they
are an inspiration for us. They are our heroes and
heroines, you might say, because when we read their
stories (when we read the story of Milarepa, for example), rather than feeling intimidated, we identify
with it all along. We see ourselves in every episode;
we realize that it's possible to keep going and never
give up. We feel devotion toward the lineage of people who have worked so hard to make it easier for us.
Sometimes you meet one particular teacher who
seems to personify that for you, and then you also
have a guru toward whom to feel devotion. It's as if
these men and women hand down a lineage of gratitude and fearlessness and cheerfulness and vision.
And they're just like us, except that we sometimes
lose heart. The fact that there are these examples
makes us tremendously grateful and devoted to these
people. It gives us some sense of spirit that we also
could follow along in that lineage. Then what *we* do

to recognize our own precious human birth can be an inspiration for everybody else.

In the early seventies a friend kept telling me, "Whatever you do, don't try to make those feelings go away." His advice went on: "Anything you can learn about working with your sense of discouragement or your sense of fear or your sense of bewilderment or your sense of feeling inferior or your sense of resentment—anything you can do to work with those things—do it, please, because it will be such an inspiration to other people." That was really good advice. So when I would start to become depressed, I would remember, "Now wait a minute. Maybe I just have to figure out how to rouse myself genuinely, because there are a lot of people suffering like this, and if I can do it, they can do it." I felt a sense of interconnectedness. "If a shmuck like me can do it, anybody can do it." That's what I used to say, that if a miserable person like me—who's completely caught up in anger and depression and betrayal—if I can do it, then anyone can do it, so I'm going to try. That was good advice that helped me to realize my precious human birth.

The second reminder is impermanence. Life is very brief. Even if we live to be a hundred, it's very brief. Also, its length is unpredictable. Our lives are impermanent. I myself have, at the most, thirty more years to live, maybe thirty-five, but that would be tops. Maybe I have only twenty more years to live. Maybe I don't even have one more day to live. It's sobering to me to think that I don't have all that long left. It makes me feel that I want to use it well. If you realize that you don't have that many more years to live and if you live your life as if you actually had only a day left, then the sense of impermanence heightens that feeling of preciousness and gratitude. Traditionally it's said that once you are born, you immediately start dying. I remember that in Boulder, every year the Hare Krishna people put up a display of life-sized figures starting with a newborn baby, through all the stages of life. You couldn't help but identify with this figure getting bigger and stronger, in the prime of life, until the whole thing starts going downhill and the figure is shown getting older, with the final one a corpse. You don't even know if you're going to have the privilege of going through that whole process. Even if you do, impermanence is very real.

When you're depressed, you may say to yourself, "Why bother to sit? Why bother to find out, for my own sake and for the sake of others, what this depression is about? Why does it drag me down? How come the sky was so blue yesterday and now everything is so gray? How come everyone was smiling at me yesterday and now they're all frowning at me? How come yesterday I felt like I was doing everything right and today it seems I'm doing everything wrong? How come? How come? How come?" If you're alone in retreat, you still get depressed. There's no one to blame it on; it's just this feeling that happens. You ask yourself, what is it? What is it? What is it? I want to know. How can I rouse myself? What can I do that's not completely habitual? How can I get out of this rut?

How do we stop the habitualness of our process? The teachings say, "Well, that's why we sit. That's what mindfulness is about. Look carefully. Pay attention to details." Remembering impermanence motivates you to go back and look at the teachings, to see what they tell you about how to work with your life, how to rouse yourself, how to cheer up, how to work with emotions. Still, sometimes you'll read and read and you can't find the answer anywhere. But then someone on a bus will tell you, or you'll find it in the middle of a movie, or maybe even in a commercial on TV. If you really have these questions, you'll find the answers everywhere. But if you don't have a question, there's certainly no answer.

Impermanence means that the essence of life is fleeting. Some people are so skillful at their mindfulness practice that they can actually see each and every little movement of mind—changing, changing, changing. They can also feel body changing, changing, changing. It's absolutely amazing. The heart pumps blood all the time and the blood keeps going and the food gets digested and the whole thing happens. It's amazing and it's very impermanent. Every time you travel in a car, that might be the end. If you get really paranoid, impermanence can drive you crazy because you're scared to step off the curb, you're scared to go out of your house. You realize how dangerous life is. It's good to realize how dangerous it is because that makes the sense of impermanence real. It is good to realize that you will die, that death is right there on your shoulder all the time. Many religions have meditations on death to let it penetrate our thick skulls that life doesn't last forever. It might be over in the next instant! Sometimes it's said that the end of every out-breath is actually *the* end; the opportunity is there to die completely. Suzuki Roshi gave the instructions, "Sit still. Don't anticipate. Just be willing to die over and over again." Let that be a reminder. Being willing to die over and over again heightens the first reminder, the sense of gratitude and preciousness. Impermanence can teach you a lot about how to cheer up. Sometimes let it scare you. It is said, "Practice as if your hair were on fire." It's okay if it scares you. Fear can make you start asking a lot of questions. If it doesn't get you down, it's going to start you wondering, "What's this fear? Where did it come from? What am I scared of?" Maybe you're scared of the most exciting things you have yet to learn. Impermanence is a great reminder.

The third reminder is karma: every action has a result. One could give a whole seminar on the law of karma. But fundamentally, in our everyday life, it's a reminder that it's important how we live. Particularly it's important at the level of mind. Every time you're willing to acknowledge your thoughts, let them go, and come back to the freshness of the present moment, you're sowing seeds of wakefulness in your unconscious. After a while what comes up is a more wakeful, more open thought. You're conditioning yourself toward openness rather than sleepiness. You might find yourself caught, but you can extricate yourself by how you use your mind, how you actually are willing to come back just to nowness, the immediacy of the moment. Every time you're willing to do that, you're sowing seeds for your own future, cultivating this innate fundamental wakefulness by aspiring to let go of the habitual way you proceed and to do something fresh. Basically this is letting go of thoughts, the churning of thoughts, and coming back to the present moment.

In one of our chants we say, "Whatever arises is fresh, the essence of realization. Grant your blessings so that my meditation is free from conceptions." Freshness here means willingness to sit up if you're slouching. If you want to stay in bed all day with the covers over your head, it means willingness to get up and take a shower with really good soap, to go down to the drugstore and buy something that smells good, to iron your shirt, shine your shoes, whatever it takes to perk up. It means doing whatever it takes to counteract your desire to throw everything on the floor, push it under the bed, not wash, just dive into this darkness. When these feelings come on, it does feel as if the whole world is collaborating with your own state of mind, acting as a mirror. Darkness seems to be everywhere. People are irritated at you, everything is closing in. Trying to cheer yourself up isn't easy, and sometimes it feels hypocritical, like going against the grain. But the reminder is that if you want to change your habitual stuckness, you're the only one who can do it.

I'm not telling you what to do, I'm just talking about seeing how you always do the same habitual things when bad feelings—uneasiness, depression, fear—start coming up. You always do the same thing; you shut down in some habitual, very old way. According to the law of karma, every action has a result. If you stay in bed all day with the covers over your head, if you overeat for the millionth time in your life, if you get drunk, if you get stoned, you know that's going to depress you and make you more discouraged, if it's just this habitual thing that you think is going to make you feel better. The older you get, the more you know how it just makes you feel more wretched. The law of karma says, "Well, how do you want to feel tomorrow, next week, next year, five years from now, ten years from now?" It's up to you how to use your life. It doesn't mean that you have to be the best one at cheering up, or that your habitual tendencies never get the better of you. It just has to do with this sense of reminding yourself. Sometimes you can say, "Couldn't care less," but after the fourth day of lying under the sheets in your dirty, smelly clothes with your socks on, with the empty bottle next to the bed—whatever the scenario is—you say, "Maybe I should go out and buy a new shirt and take a shower and go and look at the ocean or walk in the mountains or make a nice meal or do *something* to uplift my situation, to cheer myself up." Even though we may feel very heavy-hearted, instead of eating poison, we can go out and buy the best filet mignon or whatever it might be—in my case, the best peach.

The law of karma is that we sow the seeds and we reap the fruit. To remember that can be extremely helpful. So when you find yourself in a dark place where you've been countless, countless times, you can think, "Maybe it's time to get a little golden spade and dig myself out of this place." I remember my first interview with my teacher, Chögyam Trungpa, Rinpoche, very well, because I was somehow hesitant to talk to him about what was really the problem in my life. Instead, I wasted the whole interview chattering. Every once in a while he said, "How's your meditation?" and I said, "Oh, fine," and then just chattered on. When it was over, I blurted out, "I'm having this terrible time and I'm full of anger and blah-blah-blah," in the last half-second. Rinpoche walked me toward the door and said, "Well, what that feels like is a big wave that comes along and knocks you down. You find yourself lying on the bottom of the ocean with your face in the sand, and even though all the sand is going up your nose and into your mouth and your eyes and ears, you stand up and you begin walking again. Then the next wave comes and knocks you down. The waves just keep coming, but each time you get knocked down, you stand up and keep walking. After a while, you'll find that the waves appear to be getting smaller."

That's how karma works. If you keep lying there, you'll drown, but you don't even have the privilege of dying. You just live with the sense of drowning all the time. So don't get discouraged and think, "Well, I got out of bed, I took a shower. How come I'm not living in a Walt Disney movie now? I thought I was going to turn into Snow White. I thought I was going to live happily ever after. The prince kissed me; I woke up. How come I'm not living happily ever after?" The waves just keep coming and knocking you down, but you stand up again and with some sense of rousing yourself, standing up. As Rinpoche said, "After a while, you find that the waves seem to be getting smaller." That's really what happens. That's how karma works. So let that be a reminder. It's precious and it's brief and you can use it well.

Here's another story about Rinpoche going to see his teacher, Jamgon Kongtrul of Sechen. Rinpoche said that on this particular morning when he went in, Jamgon Kongtrul held up an object made of a beauti-

ful white silvery metal that glimmered in the sun,
with a long handle and something like prongs at the
top. Jamgon Kongtrul said that it had been sent to
him from England. Rinpoche came over and sat
down and they looked at it. Jamgon Kongtrul said,
"It's for eating," and when the attendants brought the
food, he took the four prongs, put them into the piece
of food, held them up, put it into his mouth, and
said, "This is how they eat with this over there. They
put it into the food and then the food sticks to these
four prongs and then they put it into their mouth."
Rinpoche looked at this and thought it was very inge-
nious, this object. Then Jamgon Kongtrul said to
him, "Someday you're going to meet the people who
make these things, and you're going to work with
them. It's not going to be easy, because you're going
to find that they're more interested in staying asleep
than in waking up." That's what he said about us. So
when you realize that's true about yourself, remind
yourself that it's up to you whether you actually experience gratitude and the preciousness of your life,
the fleetingness and the rareness of it, or whether
you become more resentful and harsh and embit-
tered and feel more and more cheated. It's up to you
how the law of karma all works out.

Finally, the fourth reminder is the futility of continuing to spin around on this treadmill that is traditionally called samsara. Someone once said that she
felt as if she were on a record that just kept going

round and round; she had got stuck in this groove, and every time she went around, the groove got deeper and deeper. I've also heard people say that sometimes, when they hear themselves speak, they feel as if they're a tape recorder playing the same tape over and over and over. They get sick of it, but somehow they just keep playing it anyway because there is a funny little identity there that gives them some kind of security, painful though it may be. That's samsara.

The essence of samsara is this tendency that we have to seek pleasure and avoid pain, to seek security and avoid groundlessness, to seek comfort and avoid discomfort. The basic teaching is that that is how we keep ourselves miserable, unhappy, and stuck in a very small, limited view of reality. That is how we keep ourselves enclosed in a cocoon. Out there are all the planets and all the galaxies and vast space, but you're stuck in this cocoon, or maybe you're inside a capsule, like a vitamin pill. Moment after moment, you are deciding that you would rather stay in that capsule. You would rather remain a vitamin pill than experience the pain of stepping out into that big space. Life in that capsule is cozy and secure. We've gotten it all together. It's safe, it's predictable, it's convenient, and it's trustworthy. We know when we walk into our house exactly where the furniture is, and it's the way we like it. We know we have all the appliances we need and we have the clothes we like. If we feel ill at ease, we just fill in those gaps. Our mind is always seeking zones of safety. We're in this zone of safety and that's what we consider life, getting it all together, security. Death is losing that. That's what we fear, that's what makes us anxious. You could call death an embarrassment—feeling awkward and off the mark. Being totally confused and not knowing which way to turn could also describe death, which we fear so much. We want to know what's happening. The mind is always seeking zones of safety, and these zones of safety are continually falling apart. Then we scramble to get another zone of safety back together again. We spend all our energy and waste our lives trying to re-create these zones of safety, which are always falling apart. That's samsara.

The opposite of samsara is when all the walls fall down, when the cocoon completely disappears and we are totally open to whatever may happen, with no withdrawing, no centralizing into ourselves. That is what we aspire to, the warrior's journey. That's what stirs us and inspires us: leaping, being thrown out of the nest, going through the initiation rites, growing up, stepping into something that's uncertain and un-known. From that point of view, death becomes this comfort and this security and this cocoon and this vitamin pill-ness. That's death. Samsara is preferring death to life. The fourth reminder is to remember that. When you find yourself with these old, familiar feelings of anxiety because your world is falling apart and you're not measuring up to your image of yourself and everybody is irritating you beyond words because no one is doing what you want and everyone is wrecking everything and you feel terrible about yourself and you don't like anybody else and your whole life is fraught with emotional misery and confusion and conflict, at that point just remember that you're going through all this emotional upheaval because your coziness has just been, in some small or large way, addressed. Basically, you *do* prefer life and warriorship to death.

Hopefully these four traditional reminders—precious human birth, the truth of impermanence, the law of karma, which is cause and effect, and the futility of continuing to prefer death to life—will help you and me for the rest of our lives, whether we are leaving here or staying on here, to wake up. So have a good journey home, and always remember—never give up!

BIBLIOGRAPHY

Hanh, Thich Nhat. *A Guide to Walking Meditation*. Berkeley, Calif.: Parallax Press, 1985.

Neihardt, John G. *Black Elk Speaks*. Lincoln: University of Nebraska Press, 1988.

Suzuki, Shunryu. *Zen Mind, Beginner's Mind*. New York and Tokyo: Weatherhill, 1970.

Trungpa, Chögyam. *Born in Tibet*. Boston: Shambhala Publications, 1985.

———. *Cutting Through Spiritual Materialism*. Boston and London: Shambhala Publications, 1987.

———. *First Thought, Best Thought: 108 Poems*. Boulder and London: Shambhala Publications, 1983.

———. *Shambhala: The Sacred Path of the Warrior*. Boston and London: Shambhala Publications, 1984, 1988.

RESOURCES

For information about meditation instruction or to find a practice center near you, please contact one of the following:

Shambhala International
1084 Tower Road
Halifax, NS
Canada B3H 2Y5
phone: (902) 425-4275
fax: (902) 423-2750
website: www.shambhala.org (This website contains information about the more than one hundred centers affiliated with Shambhala.)

Shambhala Europe
Kartaüserwall 20
D 50678 Cologne, Germany
phone: 49-221-31024-00
fax: 49-221-31024-50
e-mail: europe@shambhala.org
website: www.shambhala-europe.org

Karmê Chöling
369 Patneaude Lane
Barnet, VT 05821

phone: (802) 633-2384
fax: (802) 633-3012
e-mail: karmecholing@shambhala.org

Shambhala Mountain Center
4921 Country Road 68c
Red Feather Lakes, CO 80545
phone: (970) 881-2184
fax: (970) 881-2909
e-mail: pmsc@shambhala.org

Gampo Abbey
Pleasant Bay, NS
Canada BOE 2PO
phone: (902) 224-2752
e-mail: office@gampoabbey.org

Naropa University is the only accredited, Buddhist-inspired university in North America. For more information, contact:

Naropa University
2130 Arapahoe Avenue
Boulder, CO 80302
phone: (303) 444-0202
website: www.naropa.edu

Audio and videotape recordings of talks and seminars
by Pema Chödrön are available from:

Great Path Tapes and Books
330 East Van Hoesen Boulevard
Portage, MI 49002
phone: (616) 384-4167
fax: (415) 946-3475
e-mail: greatpath@pemachodrontapes.com
website: www.pemachodrontapes.com

Kalapa Recordings
1084 Tower Road
Halifax, NS
Canada B3H 2Y5
phone: (902) 420-1118, ext. 19
fax: (902) 423-2750
e-mail: shop@shambhala.org
website: www.shambhalashop.com

Sounds True
735 Walnut Street
Boulder, CO 80302
phone: (800) 333-9185
website: www.soundstrue.com

Cards printed with each of the mind-training slogans,
as well as a poster for use in one's practice, are available from:

Samadhi Store
Karmê Chöling
R.R. 1, Box 3
Barnet, VT 05821
phone: (800) 331-7751
e-mail: order@samadhicushions.com

Ziji Catalog
9148 Kerry Road
Boulder, CO 80303
phone: (800) 565-8470
e-mail: ziji@csd.net

Drala Books and Gifts
1567 Grafton Street
Halifax, NS
Canada B3J 2C3
phone: (902) 422-2504

The *Shambhala Sun* is a bimonthly Buddhist magazine founded by Chögyam Trungpa Rinpoche. For a subscription or sample copy, contact:

Shambhala Sun
P.O. Box 3377

Champlain, NY 12919-9868
phone (toll free): (877) 786-1950
website: www.shambhalasun.com

Buddhadharma: The Practitioner's Quarterly is an in-depth, practice-oriented journal offering teachings from all Buddhist traditions. For a subscripton or sample copy, contact:

Buddhadharma
P.O. Box 3377
Champlain, NY 12919-9871
phone (toll free): (877) 786-1950
website: www.thebuddhadharma.com

SHAMBHALA LIBRARY

The Art of Peace, by Morihei Ueshiba.
Edited by John Stevens.

The Art of War: The Denma Translation, by Sun Tzu.
Translated by the Denma Translation Group.

The Art of Worldly Wisdom, by Baltasar Gracián.

Bhagavad Gita, translated by Eknath Easwaran.

The Book of Five Rings, by Miyamoto Musashi.
Translated by Thomas Cleary.

The Book of Tea, by Kakuzo Okakura.

Bushido, by Inazo Nitobe.

*Cold Mountain Poems: Zen Poems of Han Shan,
Shih Te, and Wang Fan-chih*, translated by
J. P. Seaton.

Comfortable with Uncertainty, by Pema Chödrön.

Cutting Through Spiritual Materialism,
by Chögyam Trungpa.

The Dhammapada, translated by Gil Fronsdal.

Erotic Love Poems from India: A Translation of the
Amarushataka, by Andrew Schelling.

The Gospel of Thomas, translated by Stevan Davies.

I Ching: The Book of Change, by Cheng Yi. Translated by Thomas Cleary.

Love Poems from the Japanese, translated by Kenneth Rexroth. Edited by Sam Hamill.

Lovingkindness: The Revolutionary Art of Happiness, by Sharon Salzberg.

Mastering the Art of War, translated by Thomas Cleary.

Meditation in Action, by Chögyam Trungpa.

The Myth of Freedom and the Way of Meditation, by Chögyam Trungpa.

Nature and Other Writings, by Ralph Waldo Emerson. Edited by Peter Turner.

New Seeds of Contemplation, by Thomas Merton.

No Man Is an Island, by Thomas Merton.

The Places That Scare You, by Pema Chödrön.

The Poetry of Zen, edited and translated by Sam Hamill and J. P. Seaton.

The Rumi Collection: An Anthology of Translations of Mevlâna Jalâluddin Rumi. Edited by Kabir Helminski.

The Sabbath: Its Meaning for Modern Man, by Abraham Joshua Heschel.

Sailing Alone around the World,
by Captain Joshua Slocum.

Shambhala: The Sacred Path of the Warrior, by
Chögyam Trungpa. Edited by Carolyn Rose Gimian.

Siddhartha: A New Translation, by Hermann Hesse.
Translated by Sherab Chödzin Kohn.

*Start Where You Are: A Guide to Compassionate
Living,* by Pema Chödrön.

Tao Teh Ching, by Lao Tzu. Translated by
John C. H. Wu.

Teachings of the Buddha, edited by Jack Kornfield.

*The Tibetan Book of the Dead: The Great Liberation
through Hearing in the Bardo,* translated with
commentary by Francesca Fremantle
and Chögyam Trungpa.

Training the Mind and Cultivating Loving-Kindness,
by Chögyam Trungpa.

Walden, by Henry David Thoreau.

The Way of the Bodhisattva, by Shantideva.
Translated by the Padmakara Translation Group.

The Way of Chuang Tzu, by Thomas Merton.

*When Things Fall Apart: Heart Advice
for Difficult Times,* by Pema Chödrön.

The Wisdom of the Desert: Sayings from the Desert Fathers of the Fourth Century, by Thomas Merton.

Zen Mind, Beginner's Mind, by Shunryu Suzuki.